*Centre for Educational Research and Innovation (CERI)*

# EVALUATING EDUCATIONAL PROGRAMMES
## THE NEED AND THE RESPONSE

A collection of resource materials prepared by

Robert E. STAKE

Centre for Instructional Research
and Curriculum Evaluation
University of Illinois at Urbana Champaign

ORGANISATION FOR ECONOMIC CO-OPERATION AND DEVELOPMENT

1976

The Organisation for Economic Co-operation and Development (OECD) was set up under a Convention signed in Paris on 14th December, 1960, which provides that the OECD shall promote policies designed:

— to achieve the highest sustainable economic growth and employment and a rising standard of living in Member countries, while maintaining financial stability, and thus to contribute to the development of the world economy;
— to contribute to sound economic expansion in Member as well as non-member countries in the process of economic development;
— to contribute to the expansion of world trade on a multilateral, non-discriminatory basis in accordance with international obligations.

The Members of OECD are Australia, Austria, Belgium, Canada, Denmark, Finland, France, the Federal Republic of Germany, Greece, Iceland, Ireland, Italy, Japan, Luxembourg, the Netherlands, New Zealand, Norway, Portugal, Spain, Sweden, Switzerland, Turkey, the United Kingdom and the United States.

*The Development Centre of the Organisation for Economic Co-operation and Development was established by decision of the OECD Council on 23rd October 1962.*

*The purpose of the Centre is to bring together the knowledge and experience available in Member countries of both economic development and the formulation and execution of general policies of economic aid; to adapt such knowledge and experience to the actual needs of countries or regions in the process of development and to put the results at the disposal of the countries by appropriate means.*

*The Centre has a special and autonomous position within the OECD which enables it to enjoy scientific independence in the execution of its task. Nevertheless, the Centre can draw upon the experience and knowledge available in the OECD in the development field.*

\* \* \*

The opinions expressed and arguments employed in this publication are the responsibility of the author and do not necessarily represent those of the OECD.

© OECD, 1976.
Queries concerning permissions or translation rights should be addressed to:
Director of Information, OECD
2, rue André-Pascal, 75775 PARIS CEDEX 16, France.

## TABLE OF CONTENTS

Preface . . . . . . . . . . . . . . . . . . . . . . . . . . . .  5

BACKGROUND . . . . . . . . . . . . . . . . . . . . . . . . . .  6

Chapter I
    THE PURPOSE AND LIMITATIONS OF THE REPORT . . . . . . . .  7

Chapter II
    HOW CERTAIN PEOPLE RESPONDED TO THE NEED TO EVALUATE
    EDUCATIONAL PROGRAMMES

    1. How Government Officials and other Programme Sponsors
       have responded . . . . . . . . . . . . . . . . . . . . 12
    2. How Educators have responded . . . . . . . . . . . . . 14
    3. How Researchers have responded . . . . . . . . . . . . 16

Chapter III
    THE METHODS OF EVALUATING

    1. The most common Dimensions for classifying Evaluation
       Designs . . . . . . . . . . . . . . . . . . . . . . . . 18
    2. Nine Evaluation Approaches . . . . . . . . . . . . . . 21
    3. The Costs of Evaluating . . . . . . . . . . . . . . . . 27

Chapter IV
    NEGOTIATION OF AGREEMENTS TO DO EVALUATION STUDIES

    1. Issues for Consideration . . . . . . . . . . . . . . . 31
    2. Checklist for Negotiating an Agreement to evaluate an
       Educational Programme . . . . . . . . . . . . . . . . . 35
    3. How Administrators have responded to Nine Key Quesions 37
    4. How Researchers have responded to Seven Key Questions  52
    5. Three Hypothetical Conversations . . . . . . . . . . . 64

Appendix
    BIBLIOGRAPHY . . . . . . . . . . . . . . . . . . . . . . 85

PREFACE

CERI, since its inception in 1969, has concerned itself with change in education; with the mechanisms that might bring it about, with the organisational structures that will nurture it, and with the nature of changes in content and method in the curriculum itself. Time and again one insistent question has emerged: how successful have the changes been?

The objectives of education are so manifold, the means by which they are achieved so interrelated, and the manifestations of success so difficult to measure - even to observe - that evaluation has come to be seen as necessarily complex and often imprecise in its findings. Yet if sound judgements are to be made, a sound basis of information is essential.

This report clarifies and may throw light on the problems involved, and points the way to possible solutions.

J.R. GASS
Director
Centre for Educational
Research and Innovation

## BACKGROUND

In November 1973 CERI launched a project on "New Approaches to Evaluation of Educational Programmes". In the previous years most of the work on innovation in education had posed the problem "how does the administrator know whether or not an innovation, introduced experimentally, is worth generalizing?" It is this question that the project has made central to its work. The stress has been less on the major policy changes, such as the structural alteration of a system to comprehensive education, and more on the consequent innovations in content, method and organisation in the educational programmes that arise from them.

Particular stress has been put on the process by which the administrator decides what information he wants and then commissions the necessary evaluation study. However, this has involved also a study of the different styles of evaluation and some consideration of the methods by which the results could be communicated.

This report is the work of Professor Robert Stake of the University of Illinois at Urbana-Champaign aided by experts from many countries and by post-graduate students. He was able to spend a sabbatical year, preceding the writing of this report, in Sweden and the United Kingdom. To help in the process CERI organised an international Conference at Liège, hosted by the Belgian authorities, which used much of the first draft as background materials. A document, CERI/NAE/75.01, which summarizes the work that went into and emerged from this Conference is available on demand.

To be appreciated fully, this report should be read in conjunction with the document, free on demand from CERI, entitled "Case Studies in the Evaluation of Educational Programmes". These were collected and edited by Professor Stake.

Chapter I

THE PURPOSE AND LIMITATIONS OF THE REPORT

This report has been prepared as a survey of the developments in educational programme (1) evaluation in the middle 1970's. It is expected primarily to be of use to persons who will have responsibility for commissioning and implementing evaluation studies. Most of those people will be government officials but some will hold positions in schools, in industry, with philanthropic foundations or will be members of special councils. It will be their responsibility during the remainder of the 1970's to be the commissioners of evaluation, to provide the initiative and direction for evaluation studies.

The report is written also for evaluators who will carry out the new studies. Many of them will not have previous experience in an evaluative study of national scope - there are not many people in the world who have. Some prospective evaluators will have had extensive experience in educational research, and the differences between research and evaluation may be difficult for them to understand. Some prospective evaluators will have had experience in teaching or administration, and their inclinations to move from evaluation into decision making for the programme may be a problem. They and other researchers and educators may find useful information in this report, but it has been written mostly with the education official in mind.

The greatest particular responsibility considered in this report is that of getting the evaluative study started in a proper manner. The issues to be discussed by officials and prospective evaluators prior to making an agreement and the considerations that might be included specifically in that agreement are given special attention.

It is apparent that officials and evaluators have different expectations about what studies can and should accomplish. Although their differences are never completely resolved, thorough discussions can help. It is not assumed that the contract that fixes the details most rigidly will serve both parties best for substantial

---
1) "Programme" in this report is used as a portmanteau word to cover the content, method and frame of a learning system.

changes in expectation and need will often occur during the conduct of the study. It is the purpose of this document to alert the reader to some of the issues that may require planning and formal agreement.

There are, of course, many different evaluation responsibilities. In this report attention has been largely given to the establishment of a large-scale, perhaps national, evaluative study, probably to be conducted once only rather than on a recurring basis. No effort was made here to examine the problems of establishing better procedures for monitoring ordinary operations in the schools. No effort was made here to examine the problems of prescribing evaluation requirements to be carried out by project officers or their subcontractors, in special programmes such as in the Head Start Program in the U.S.A. or in the state-funded innovative projects in Hesse, West Germany.

Emphasis is given to the evaluation of a particular programme, usually an already operating programme, rather than to the evaluation of a particular issue. Two examples of issues are changing selective and special schools into comprehensive schools for all pupils and using a special alphabet to teach reading. Issues are important aspects of programme evaluation; but if the focus is on the issue rather than on the programme, more traditional educational-research methods are likely to be appropriate.

It is not suggested in this report that education has not been evaluated heretofore. Each teacher, each administrator throughout the years has been evaluating. Informal, personal evaluation should be no less important at a time when formal evaluative research studies are becoming important. The new studies provide information to persons who are not in a position to make personal observations or who do not have good ways of combining informal information from many schools. The new studies provide an additional kind of information about large programmes, potentially more accurate, more objective, and more valid for the purpose on hand. The new studies are a response to an emerging need.

Attendance and fiscal records, and in some countries pupil test records, have long been kept. These records are more transportable. They can be accumulated and examined by a distant educational official or programme sponsor. But such records alone leave their readers poorly acquainted with the accomplishment and the problems of the educational programme.

It is not supposed that all local information and all problems need the attention of distant officials. But some additional information is sought. There is a quickly increasing belief that more information on school proceedings and on the evidence of strength and weakness of those proceedings is essential to the proper governance of education.

As this report has been written by an author whose experience is largely in one country for readers in many countries, and who, inevitably, has his own point of view, it has certain limitations.

It is recognised that the need and responsibility will be different in each country, just as the history and present circumstance are different in each. The American experience is unique - an unrepresentative past and a most uncertain guide to the future. Yet it is the experience cited mostly in this report - not chosen on its merit but because, like Mt. Everest, it is there, and because it is the experience most familiar to the author and others who helped prepare this report. It is hoped that the fullness of their descriptions will permit readers to ascertain the relevance of the findings, the models, and the advice contained herein to the present circumstances and to future evaluation work in their countries.

In America formal educational programme evaluation has been greatly influenced by strong professional commitment to standardized testing, by an expectation that local boards of education and parent groups will help determine instructional objectives and curricular priorities, and by the development of commercial agencies for the contracting of large-scale studies such as the evaluation of federally funded projects. Observers such as Ernest House and David Cohen (1) have recognised the highly political nature of the demand in the United States for evaluation of education. Such demands are to be heard wherever legislatures meet and are common phrasing in educational tracts distributed both by reform and establishmentarian groups. In recent years, particularly in the face of ballooning costs, demands for evidence of accountability of the schools to their communities have been widespread and even strident. Although many completed evaluation studies fell short of their promise, the demand for evaluation in the United States has not diminished.

The author has worked with designs and procedures for evaluation at the local school-district level, at the state level, and at the federal level for a little over ten years. His experience is largely limited to American work - and his orientation has been somewhat uncommon even there. As the listings of Section III indicate, he has promoted a relatively naturalistic, process-oriented approach to evaluation. Readers who favour a more psychometric, experimental, or product-oriented approach may find the report unduly biased. It is hoped that all readers will take these personal commitments and limitations into account and even be stimulated to further study of

---

1) See Ernest R. House (Ed.), School Evaluation: The Politics and Process, Berkeley: McCutchan, 1973; and David K. Cohen, "Politics and Research - Evaluation of Large-Scale Programs," Review of Educational Research, 1970, 40 (2), 213-238.

their implications. A bibliography accompanying the matrix in Section III should be helpful in identifying the risks and potential payoff of this and alternative approaches to the evaluation of educational programmes.

The limitations of this report cannot be listed in full, partly due to the finite length of the report; but one additional limitation requires mention. The report is limited by the point of view that responsibility for research upon educational affairs should be aggressively assumed by educators. This is not to say that citizens and elected officials should not investigate these affairs. This is not to say that scholars from the many learned disciplines should not study education. Nor should educational researchers disdain the use of concepts, methods, or advice of researchers from other fields. It is a point of view that assumes that educators must take primary responsibility for the evaluation of educational programmes.

The education profession has rather successfully maintained control of educational research. Few researchers are full-time teachers or administrators, but most consider themselves members of the profession rather than members of a discipline such as psychology or economics. Their work is generally in good repute - only a few critics find it essentially without merit.(1) It is the educational researcher who is most frequently asked to direct an evaluation study, and it is he who writes most of the treatises on how it should be done. Those writings do not always inspire confidence that the profession can evaluate its own work. A widely respected American researcher commented:(2)

> "...we have reached the end of an era that should never have happened. There is nothing more tedious than having a collection of miscellaneous essays, each one decorated with the author's "systematic" table or flowchart, all taking in each other's washing. The point of diminishing returns in essays on educational evaluation was passed in 1968 or 1970.
> "...none of us thought to ask whether educational evaluation was a field by itself distinct from other evaluation of social systems. There had in fact been a fairly substantial evaluation movement in the postwar years that was mostly in the hands of applied sociologists. Without any insistence that they made great advances, I think it was a mistake for us to proceed with a parochial discussion, to develop our own jargon, and to talk only with a small group of insiders.

---

1) See Daniel Kallos, "On Educational Scientific Research," Report No. 36, Institute of Education, University of Lund, Sweden, April 1973.
2) Personal correspondence to the author, February 11, 1974.

> "...our isolation has been increasingly damaging as work in evaluation shifted in the middle '60s to the evaluation of program and policies, as distinct from the evaluation of types of classroom practice. . . . Few of us have been able...to participate constructively in the debates about how future evaluation money is to be spent. And this is because that front has been manned by the sociologists, economists, and systems analysts."

Evaluators should avoid an over-attention to model-building and the tendency toward preachment and should not abdicate their responsibility to sociologists, economists, and systems analysts. The main purpose of many educational evaluation studies will be to increase the understanding educators have of particular educational programmes. The responsibility evaluators have to be of service to educators usually requires a thorough understanding of education as a profession, as an art, and as a social service. Few social scientists can or care to build upon that understanding.

Basic research on educational issues should continue to be done by social scientists as well as by educational researchers. Multidisciplinary studies should continue to be encouraged. However, programme evaluation studies, this report assumes, will usually be of most value to education officials when developed around the educational issues found in the programme rather than around the social science issues. The advantages and disadvantages of this approach should become more apparent in the several sections of this report.

Chapter II

## HOW CERTAIN PEOPLE HAVE RESPONDED TO THE NEED TO EVALUATE EDUCATIONAL PROGRAMMES

### 1. HOW GOVERNMENT OFFICIALS AND OTHER PROGRAMME SPONSORS HAVE RESPONDED

There are not many government officials and patrons who fail to see a need for formal evaluation. It is they who are asking for the studies, supporting the necessary budget requests, and expressing an optimism about how useful the results will be. They are anguished by the decisions that must be made on too little information. They recognise that limited funds must be split among competing needs. They plead for evaluation studies to help identify programme costs and accomplishments. Jimmy Carter, Governor of the State of Georgia, said:(1)

> "We in government are faced with the problem of determining the 'ideal' level of services within constraints of available revenues. . . . On what basis and toward what end will these programs be directed and at what cost? This question can only be answered through an evaluation system for social services programs."

and Henry Ford II of the Ford Motor Company said:(2)

> "...the government has no effective mechanism for measuring the costs and results of prior legislation against its goals. . . . In every decision we must weigh the benefits to society against the costs to society, and let the balance dictate the choice."

Not all officials and administrators are enthusiastic about evaluation; but in the main they are more positively inclined than even the evaluators.

---

1) See Jimmy Carter, "Reply to Position Paper," Evaluation, Spring 1974, Special Issue, 6-7.
2) See Henry Ford II, "Reply to Position Paper," Evaluation, Spring 1974, Special Issue, 8-12.

Some officials have had favourable experiences with evaluative research, but usually the support sponsors give is based on hope rather than experience. Few sponsors have had either good or bad experience with formal programme evaluation studies. They become painfully aware of how little is known about their programmes, how complex the problems are, and how elusive the solutions. They are, as a group, highly conscientious about the effectiveness of the programmes, about doing what is best for the constituencies of those programmes. Their summons to use rational management methods to improve those programmes is energized in bureau after bureau, in agency after agency, by benevolent concern and long hours of preparation.

Quite frequently the commitment to evaluate is coupled with a commitment to a technological approach for management. Folk wisdom and intuitive decision making are found wanting, planning and specification are found worthy. The measure of good sense in these commitments varies from time to time and from place to place. There are many situations where the various costs of additional technology outweigh the benefits. But there also are many situations which lack order, precision, and rationality and for which a more technological approach to evaluation is clearly needed.

These officials in government halls and from other agencies and institutions are sensitive to the communication problems mentioned in the previous section. They know how difficult it is to find out what is going on. They know how difficult it is to inform others of what is going on. They find the need for documentation broad and compelling. They are persuaded that only those things that are written down can be shared widely and only those messages that are carefully coded can be aggregated to provide a meaningful summation across successive years and diverse locations. They support the search for documentary evidence of programme success.

Their reasoning has much to recommend it, but there are grounds for being cautious. Documentation is both costly and simplifying. The costs of keeping useful records often eat into operating costs. The records kept never reflect the full complexity of the programme, sometimes providing a simplistic picture which is easily misinterpreted. Administrators occasionally overlook these drawbacks. After all, the call for evaluation and the presence of records, the call itself and the presence itself, are testimony that the administrators are doing their job. In instances where the records are not useful, or even misleading, the blame seldom goes to the person who required them. There is a danger that officials will be more concerned about being "on record" as recognising the need for evaluation than about making a reasonable response to that need.

Official statements are made that reflect the assumption that what is good for society, that what is good for educational research is good for education, and that what is good for the evaluation of a particular programme is good for the evaluation of all of education. Thus is almost any demand for evaluation supported. These assumptions do not hold. Sometimes efforts made for the one are to the detriment of the other. Not all calls for evaluation are going to benefit education and society. The officials sometimes respond to the need with extravagant claims as to the benefits.

There is another important effect of the responses officials make. They tend to make demands that result in responsibility shifting increasingly to programme headquarters and away from the schools or projects in the field. By authenticating certain issues via interview and questionnaire, by emphasizing certain objectives through goal statements and test items, or by elevating certain expectations and standards with specific definitions in official nomenclature, responsibility for the programme shifts from the people in the field to the programme directorate. This occurs even where there are sustained efforts to use democratic expressions of purpose and to use the language of professionals in the field. Sometimes the shift is deliberate, sometimes unintended and undetected. Sometimes it is good, sometimes bad. But it happens.

The response of programme sponsors to evaluation needs is both well-reasoned and self-serving. The sponsors have their patrons, their audiences. There is a story to be passed along. The sponsors want the programme to succeed and they want to be recognised for having supported it. The situation is largely the same in a government bureau, the armed forces, a university, or a philanthropic foundation.

## 2. HOW EDUCATORS HAVE RESPONDED

Teachers, professors, and headmasters have been apprehensive about new demands for programme evaluation. They have been concerned about the success of their programmes, and they have been concerned about the increasing demands made upon those programmes. They recognise the increased involvement of distant authorities in curricular matters, and many are sceptical about the good that may come of it. Most importantly, educators recognise that any effort to evaluate the programme is likely to perceive inadequately and misrepresent at least some of it - and the chances of the programme being hurt often appear much greater than the chances of the programme being helped. In other words, there is a fear of formal evaluation; and this fear is not entirely without cause.

It is not that these educators are against evaluation. As a group they are quite ready to pass judgement on school affairs, on teacher performance, and on administrator performance and to grade students on almost everything they do. Not all of them, of course; some are quite opposed to course marks. Some are uncritical of almost anything that happens in their world. But most are evaluative.

Not surprisingly, they see little connection between the kind of professional judgement exercised in these informal evaluations and the scaling that goes on in most evaluation studies. They do not deny the subjectivity and limited experience underlying many informal decisions but do not see that it would be improved by technology. They fail to see the relevance to their programmes of most of the studies they know which have placed a premium on objectivity and systematization.

Often educators raise little or no objection to "national" or "international" studies. They volunteer their services as test administrators. They provide observations of events. They yield up their children, often as if that were the most important thing the children could be doing at that moment. There is some increasing reluctance to be so generous, but getting educator co-operation has not been a serious obstacle for evaluators.

Teacher unions and other professional organisations have started to speak out on the value of evaluation, particularly as it involves the evaluation of their members. And, of course, many evaluative studies reflect upon the contribution of teachers. The official rhetoric of the organisation usually is "pro-evaluation". Their occasional cautionary advice is well-reasoned, and they make an increasing demand that evaluation responsibility be left in the hands of educators. The response of these educator organisations seems to be shifting from silent tolerance to occasional participation in sponsorship, with some increasing restriction against unpaid service by members.

Many educators would report that they fail to see an increasing responsibility for evaluating education. They believe the responsibility today is not truly different from what it has been before. What has happened is increased publicity, increased expectations of education, and increased cost. With more people concerned, there seems to be more demand for formal evaluation; but the educators are not at all persuaded that formal evaluation should replace informal evaluation.

It is safe to say, though, that in the great majority of instances professional educators will be co-operative with well presented and reasonably modest requests for participation in evaluation studies of their schools, curricula, and pupil performances.

## 3. HOW RESEARCHERS HAVE RESPONDED

Educational researchers have responded enthusiastically — by and large — to the responsibility for evaluating programmes. They are motivated by an honest concern for the effectiveness of education and a conviction that rational study of educational processes will ultimately improve them. These words of Patricia Story, University of Cambridge, reflect that optimism and concern:[1]

> "...an evaluator's role is a complex one. He is to help with the clarification of the aims of the course, if not with their actual formulation; he has a knowledge of sampling techniques and can organize test programmes; and presumably he must be familiar with the content and teaching methods of the course he is testing, and preferably have some teaching experience. Even if the evaluator is not expected to possess or exercise all these skills, the fact remains that he needs to be a person of protean ability or at least to have very good advisers."

Researchers have looked at the schools from many vantage points. Many of them question some school goals and priorities. Many see inefficiency and unproductiveness in the pursuit of worthy goals. Underlying their criticism, whether in the laboratory or when giving national testimony, is usually a deep and enduring commitment to the profession.

The training these educational researchers have had and the company they keep reinforce their preference for a rational approach to educational management. Most of them are dubious about reliance on administrative experience as a basis for governing the schools. Many look forward to a day when decisions will be made by objective measurement and validated formulae.

Though idealistic these researchers are, they are not immune to the temptation to imply that their own expertise and styles of inquiry have been found regularly to be effective aids to policy setting and routine operations. They recommend looking at problems through the eyes of their specialties. An educational psychologist can be expected to give priority to measurements of personal talent and personality. An educational sociologist is likely to recommend role analysis and the study of community structure. An economist emphasizes costs, a historian events. It is understandable but not a reliable guide to the concepts and methods that might be most helpful.

---

1) See Patricia Story, "Cambridge School Classics Project," in Schools Council Research Studies, Evaluation in Curriculum Development: Twelve Case Studies. London: Macmillan, 1973, 36-46.

And it is to be expected that the more the researcher is called upon to conduct the evaluation or be a consultant, the more he will use it to further his own research programme and to provide training opportunities for his students. All very well, except that the well-being of the programme and the well-being of the researcher do not always lie in the same direction. The researcher is to be found, as all humans are, under a constellation of motives. Fortunately, in circumstances of programme evaluation his motives usually have an opportunity to respond in concert, supporting the use of more formal designs in order to learn more about the particular programme and, at the same time, to learn more in general about educational processes.

Most educational researchers suggest a number of ideals for the evaluation design. It should be rational. It should be preplanned and prespecified. It should operationalize concepts, not leave them abstract and vague. It should give focus to impact on students. It should provide feedback for decision making. Few would reject these as ideals, but some researchers would set lower standards in order to emphasize other design characteristics and to accomplish different aims.

The educational researcher has responded to the need for formal evaluation of educational programmes by offers of help and with an expectation that basic methods and concepts, relied on in the past, will serve well again. As is his wont, however, he has subdivided his methodological cabinet to store new evaluation models and new terms. The researcher is showing a growing awareness that the evaluation concerns of educators and programme sponsors can be a worthy challenge to his expertise and can be a justifiable priority for his attention.

A serious problem exists because different people have such different expectations of what good evaluation studies will do. The government official often is looking for information that will help him choose among competing programmes and budget requests. The educator often is looking for understanding about a particular teaching and learning situation. The researcher often is looking for broad understanding about the teaching and learning processes. A single evaluation study, even if successfully following a good design, will not satisfy such different expectations. The purpose of our next section is to examine the aims and claims for different methods of evaluating.

Chapter III

THE METHODS OF EVALUATING

No one method of evaluating educational programmes is suitable for all situations. The information needs will vary. The audiences will have different expectations and standards. The evaluators will have different styles, which in turn are more or less useful to different clients. The purpose of this section is to examine some of the differences in existing evaluation methods.

1. THE MOST COMMON DIMENSIONS FOR CLASSIFYING EVALUATION DESIGNS

The writing of Michael Scriven has been influential in identifying basic dimensions of evaluation. His paper "The Methodology of Evaluation"(1) identified six dimensions, starting with a distinction between the goal of evaluation (to indicate "worth") and the roles of evaluation (the different reasons and circumstances for which we need to know the "worth"). Blaine Worthen and James Sanders (2) created a more elaborate taxonomy of evaluation designs. For this report ideas are borrowed from both these sources but presented in a simpler and less thorough way.

Formative-Summative

The most pervading distinction Scriven made was one between evaluation studies done during the development of a programme and those done after the programme has been completed. Obviously, a developing programme has components that are completed day by day. It is difficult to distinguish between the summative evaluation of a completed component and the formative evaluation of a part of the programme. The distinction is not clear-cut.

---

1) See Michael Scriven, "The Methodology of Evaluation", AERA Monograph Series on Curriculum Evaluation, No. 1. Chicago: Rand McNally, 1967, 39-83.
2) See Blaine R. Worthen and James R. Sanders, Educational Evaluation: Theory and Practice. Worthington, Ohio: Charles A. Jones Publishing Company, 1973.

The most useful distinction here may be between the users of the evaluation findings. Elsewhere I have noted that when the cook tastes the soup it is formative evaluation and when the guest tastes the soup it is summative. The key is not so much <u>when</u> as <u>why</u>. What is the information for, for further preparation and correction or for savouring and consumption? Both lead to decision-making, but toward different decisions.

Formal-Informal

It would be foolish not to recognise the distinction between formal and informal studies, even though in this report only formal evaluation studies are being considered. Informal evaluation is a universal and abiding human act, scarcely separable from thinking and feeling. Formal evaluation is more operationalized and open to view, and less personal. It is needed when the results are to be communicated elsewhere. Of the two, the formal evaluation study is under an obligation to pass tests of accuracy, validity, credibility, and utility.

Case Particular-Generalisation

A most important distinction is between the study of a programme as a fixed and ultimate target, or the study of a programme as a representative of others. Most research is expected to be generalised in some ways: over time, over settings or over subject matters, for example. Evaluation research may be done essentially to discover the worth of the particular programme, or the worth of the general approach. Studies are perceived very differently in this regard, both by investigators and their audiences; and a large misperception is possible.

The more the study is expected to be a basis for generalisation the more the need for controls, controlled variation, or careful description of uncontrolled variation. Description is needed of the changes in time and place and persons, and in many of the ways in which generalisation may be directed. The case study undertaken for either knowledge of the particular or for generalisation is a more useful document when it provides the reader with a vivid portrayal of the setting and context of the teaching and learning.

Product-Process

Another dimension on which evaluation studies vary is as to whether they give primary attention to the outcomes of the programme or to its transactions. A study of the "product" is expected to indicate the payoff value; a study of the "process" is expected to indicate the intrinsic values of the programme. Both are needed in any effort to get at a full indication of the worth of the programme, but in any actual study only a small portion of either can be examined. Much of the argument as to preferable methods depends on the beliefs held as to which is more measurable and useful.

Descriptive-Judgmental

Many evaluators coming from a social science background define the evaluation task largely as one of providing information, with an emphasis on objective data and a de-emphasis on subjective data. Those coming from the humanities are likely to reverse the emphases. One will find some studies highly descriptive of students and settings, providing careful reports of differences and correlations, but with little direct reference to criteria of worth and value standards. And elsewhere one will find evaluation studies probing into the pluralism of values to be found in any educational setting. As with any of these dimensions, any particular study is not likely to be at one pole or the other, but to make some combination the compromise. The extremes identify a dimension on which some variation is apparent from study to study.

Preordinate-Responsive

Studies differ considerably as to how much the _issues_ of evaluation are determined by observation of activities and by realisation of concerns of participants in the programme. Preordinate studies are more oriented to objectives, hypotheses and prior expectations, mediated by the abstractions of language. Preordinate evaluators know what they are looking for and design the study so as to find it. Responsive studies are organised around phenomena encountered - often unexpectedly - as the programme goes along. (There are ways of being prespecified and responsive other than these, of course.)

In a preordinate study a relatively large portion of resources is spent on getting objectives specified in writing and developing instruments; and sometimes in providing for or controlling variation to yield more dependable statements of relationship among variables. In a responsive study a relatively large portion of resources is spent in preparing and placing observers on the scene.

Wholistic-Analytic

Studies differ also as to how much they treat the programme as a totality, recognising conceptual boundaries common to non-technical audiences. The more common social-science research approach is to concentrate on a small number of key characteristics. A case study is often used to preserve the complexity of the programme as a whole, whereas a multivariate analysis is more likely to indicate the relationships among descriptive variables.

Internal-External

An obviously important difference in evaluation studies is whether they will be conducted by personnel of the institution responsible for the programme or by outsiders. They differ as to how formal the agreement to evaluate, as to how free the evaluators are to raise issues and interpret findings, and as to how changes in plans will be negotiated.

The eight dimensions above do not result in 256 different evaluation designs. Many of the dimensions are correlated, both conceptually and in frequency-of-use. For example, an "internal" evaluation study is more likely to be formative than summative, more likely to be descriptive than judgmental. These characteristics and correlations might be particular to the places where evaluation has been most common. In new evaluation situations the key dimensions and combinations might be quite different.

## 2. NINE EVALUATION APPROACHES

Another way to look at the different ways educational programmes are evaluated is to look at typical approaches. The differences between the approaches can partly be described in terms of the dimensions just discussed, but more subtle characteristics become apparent when models or prototypes are examined.

In this section, nine approaches will be considered. The first two are very common. In any one year at least 10 per cent of American teachers and pupils are involved, at least for a few minutes, in student achievement testing or institutional self-study, as part of a formal evaluation effort. Some of the others are typical as part of informal evaluation, but uncommon as formal studies. The last two are much more rare, but increasingly mentioned by evaluation consultants. For the deeper understanding of this chapter particularly, it is advisable that it is read in conjunction with the OECD document "Case Studies in the Evaluation of Educational Programmes" which is available free on demand from CERI/OECD. References in the text to case studies are to those in that document.

Student Gain by Testing

The approach usually suggested by measurement specialists and educational psychologists is "testing to measure student gain in performance". It relies on tests developed to match prespecification of objectives or on standardized tests that match or cover programme objectives (or their correlates). Many studies are undertaken using tests developed primarily for counselling and guidance purposes. Educators in favour of highly structured curricula prefer criterion-referenced tests as a basis for measuring student gain or mastery of the task. Control groups are sometimes used. Analysis of regression or covariance is sometimes used to identify variance in student scores attributable only to the teaching. The method is found weak by some critics because the tests under-represent what education apparently does for school children and because the identification of poor learning is often not much help in identifying or correcting deficiencies in teaching.

Two of the case studies available in the companion document are primarily student-testing based, the Michigan Assessment study and the evaluation of "Follow Through". (However there is some student testing in most of the case studies here.) Both of them were set up to improve programme management and to provide information for state and national policy setting. Neither evaluation study was greatly successful in these roles. A third case study, that which resulted in the Coleman Report, used a great amount of student testing. Partly because of action by the U.S. courts the Coleman study more effectively sustained its readers' concern about government policy for schools, desegregation, and educational opportunity. Most of the "accountability laws" passed by state legislatures in the U.S. imply or mandate a student-testing approach.

Institutional Self-Study by Staff

Mostly because schools in America have, by law, a great deal of autonomy, their officers have looked for ways of evaluating them, to avoid federal and state control. Long ago they formed regional alliances, a network of schools, for the purpose of accrediting each other. A number of special professional organisations, such as the American Association of Medical Colleges and the National Council for the Accreditation of Teacher Education, moved in the same way to provide self regulation and to avoid state regulation.

The principal method of evaluation adopted by these organisations has been faculty self-study. This is not to say that the final word on any matter was left to the school's faculty, but the primary gathering of data, interpreting of problems and recommending improvements has been via the initiative and hard work of the faculty. Review by visiting committees and adherence to specifications adopted by member schools has also been common to the self-regulation process.

The self-study is sometimes used by an institution under internal pressure, without any external requirement, such as when students are protesting or when major budget changes are imminent. It is a procedure which honours the status quo, establishmentarian values. It takes a heavy toll in staff time, and is a subject in contract negotiations with some unions. It has the great value of keeping problem-solving responsibility at the site of the problem. None of the case studies gathered here illustrates this approach to programme evaluation.

Prestige Panel or Blue-Ribbon Panel

A third common evaluation approach used by governments and organisations of all kinds is the panel of leading citizens, usually people without expertise in education (or whatever the focus is), but who are held in high esteem, who have a strong sense of social responsibility, and who are respected for outstanding achievement of some kind. A group of several such people is asked to study a problem. They may follow their intuitions, or be guided by an experienced counsel or staff member. They are expected to make a very formal report, usually in a matter of weeks or months.

A well-known example of this approach is the British report on "children and their primary schools" prepared by Lady Beatrice Plowden and her committee.(1) In some countries such studies are often used as grounds for the enactment of corrective legislation. The blue-ribbon panel, also, is often the first choice among evaluation methods when matters are "in extremis" - seized upon by leaders when the institution has been greatly injured, or is immobilized by crisis.

Less sensational instances are common in the schools when a new curriculum or student policy or staff organisation is needed. A prestigious group is asked to investigate. It almost always is expected to make recommendations. In these instances the method becomes similar to the self-study approach mentioned previously. It should be noted that the distinction of the panel members permits them to use personal experience and judgment as an adjunct to and sometimes in lieu of more objective and definitive data.

None of the case studies is an example of this approach. It might be noted that, in the case of the Michigan Assessment Programme, the Michigan Educational Association, a professional organisation for teachers, sponsored a study of the state assessment by engaging a blue-ribbon panel of evaluation specialists.(2)

---

1) See Lady Beatrice Plowden et al., "A Report of the Central Advisory Committee on Children and Their Primary Schools," London: Her Majesty's Stationery Office, 1967.

2) See Ernest House, Wendall Rivers, and Daniel Stufflebeam, "Assessment of Michigan's Accountability System". Michigan Educational Association: Teacher's Voice Supplement, April 22, 1974.

## Transaction-Observation

In contrast to the student-testing approach as a (sometimes) disciplined study focusing mainly on educational outcomes, the transaction observation approach is a (sometimes) disciplined study of educational processes. Here the activities of the programme are studied, and with special attention to settings or milieu. Issues are often drawn from the proceedings rather than from theory or from goal statements.

Disciplines from which the methods of observation come include anthropology, ethnography, history and journalism. Some of these disciplines emphasize the crucial importance of reporting as well as of measuring. This evaluation approach follows that lead.

The transactions emphasized are not those between evaluator and educator, although it is the evaluator with this approach who seems to be especially sensitive to professional role relationships. This is nicely illustrated in the UNCAL case study. The transactions emphasized are those that take place in the classroom as learner encounters instructional arrangements, plus the many transactions among educators making those arrangements. Observations are made in global fashion, either by trained observers or by participants who are debriefed by trained interviewers.

The SIA evaluation is an especially good example of this approach. Several Swedish schools had completed an experimental teaching programme. The evaluation was an ad hoc study to see what had been learned. The principal attention was to what the teachers had done, with particular reference to how much the instruction was influenced by institutional and cultural frame factors. The highly political negotiations to initiate the evaluation were an instructive aspect of the study.

In the transaction-observation approach one often will find an attention to the pluralism of values in education. This is consistent with the plea made by François Hetman in a 1973 OECD document.(1) He first extracted a sentence from a Report of the (U.S.) National Academy of Sciences (1969):

> "Whatever improvement might be made in assessment systems, therefore, it is important to remember that the products of such systems ultimately represent no more than inputs into the complex network of decision-making processes, private and public, economic and political, that together mold the growth of technology and channel its integration into the social structure."

---

1) See François Hetman, <u>Society and the Assessment of Technology</u>, Paris: Organisation for Economic Co-operation and Development, 1973.

"But is this duty to fall only and exclusively to the central decision-making authorities? In a pluralistic society, such a monopoly in formulating and assessing alternative future options and courses of action may be regarded as a contradiction if not as a real danger to democracy. Hence the idea of a "competitive assessment", in other words, of such an institutional set-up as would allow different sectors of activity, organisations, groups of interest and affected parties to make assessments of their own, on the basis of their proper standpoint and scale of values."

It is not unusual to find populistic sentiment in the transaction-observation methodology.

Instructional Research

When many educational researchers are asked to recommend an evaluation approach they speak of an experimental design, with comparison of randomized treatments under controlled conditions, or as close an approximation as possible. They urge the investigator not to pass up the chance to contribute to the general knowledge about teaching and learning, sometimes paying little attention to whether or not the study is useful to the people involved in the programme.

Some authorities believe that the experimental approach is essential even to an understanding of the particular programme.

"...the small differences [educational programs] are likely to make can easily be either overestimated or missed entirely by comparing the treatment group with a non-comparable group. The only truly satisfactory way of dealing with this problem, of course, is through randomly assigned treatment and control groups."(1)

There is a great respectability to this approach, but it has come increasingly under criticism for its poor record of assistance to practitioners and policy setters. In a section (Responses of Administrators to Nine Key Questions) further on, John Nisbet is quoted reflecting concern about the educational research approach and the student-testing approach, especially in formative evaluation.

But the purpose of evaluation sometimes is to speak of summative values and to provide generalised information. Such was the field study of programmed biology materials both prepared and evaluated by Richard Anderson, and reported as a case study in this book.

---

1) From John W. Evans, "Evaluating Educational Programs - Are We Getting Anywhere?". Educational Researcher, Vol. 3, No. 8, September 1974, p. 9.

Robert F. Boruch has published an excellent bibliography (1) of particular studies and general guidelines on the evaluation of randomized experimental programmes. His references include programmes of social rehabilitation, law enforcement, socio-medical experimentation and welfare as well as education.

## Management Analysis and Social Policy Analysis

The next two approaches blend into each other but represent differences in the urgency of the findings and audiences. When an evaluative study is done to assist programme managers (to make immediate or repetitive monitoring decisions) the approach might be called Management Analysis. When the same study is done to assist policy-making, perhaps with a longer time-span, perhaps for a wide constituency or for governing board members (rather than managers) the approach might be called Social Policy Analysis. But they are similar in many respects. They both draw upon the social sciences not usually involved in educational research, management perhaps more often raising economic issues, policy-setters perhaps more often raising socio-political issues. They both draw up such economic concepts as cost-benefit analysis and productivity coefficients, and such sociological concepts as opportunity costs and work ethic.

One case study reported here which illustrates a social survey approach to policy setting is that of the Coleman study of "equal opportunity". The principal data are achievement test results but the style of analysis and the interpretations are those of the social policy analyst.

The evaluation of the Illinois Program for Gifted Children and of Ottawa's Informational Retrieval Television are both studies undertaken by the sponsors of the programme (one government, one private) to help decide whether the programmes should be expended, cut back, or changed in some ways. In both cases the officials, finding that no startling facts were likely to emerge, took action before the several years of findings were available to them.

## Goal-Free Evaluation and Adversary Evaluation

These two approaches are newcomers to the educational research scene. Michael Scriven introduced goal-free evaluation with the conversation reproduced in the next chapter. To avoid co-option he stressed keeping distance between evaluator and programme staff, even to the extent of not knowing what the staff goals were.

---

1) See Robert F. Boruch, "Bibliography: Illustrative Randomized Field Experiments for Program Planning and Evaluation". Evaluation, Volume 2, No. 1, 1974, 83-88.

Scriven's evaluator is aware of what goals are usually pursued and is supposed to be sensitive to a great range of indications that attainments were made, so the approach is not goal-free in that sense. A highly structured checklist of evidences is utilised.

The Adversary approach has several champions, most prominently Murray Levine, Thomas Owens and Robert Wolf.(1) The resources for evaluation are divided in two; part to show the shortcomings of the programme, the rest to show merit. In some cases the court of law is taken as the model, with the testimony shaped, the case made, and with cross-examination by counsels for the prosecution and the defence. The approach has an unusual command of the use of real time for decision-making, an asset that few other approaches can match.

These nine prototypes are over-simplifications of the approaches evaluators actually use. Most actual studies draw upon several styles, varying as the programme, the issues and the audiences change.

On the following page, a grid summarises the features of these nine approaches. (A bibliography of readings relevant to this will be found in the Appendix.)

Like evangelist preachers and high pressure salesmen, evaluators promote their methods. There is good and bad in each of them. The task for the consumer is to pick the method for which the things it does well are important and for which the things it does poorly are unimportant. But there is all too little agreement, all too little evidence, as to what each method does accomplish under which circumstances.

## 3. THE COSTS OF EVALUATING

An evaluation study seems to cost whatever the funding agency can afford. The experience of many evaluators indicates that the director will employ as many people as the funds will allow, once the costs of instruments, data processing, travel and administration are taken care of. A good estimate is that 80 per cent of evaluation budgets go to professional salaries.

One common procedure of funding agencies is to set aside a certain portion of the programme's operating costs for evaluation. For

---

1) See Murray Levine, "Scientific Method and the Adversary Model: Some Preliminary Suggestions", Evaluation Comment, 1973, 4(2), 1-3;
Thomas R. Owens, "Educational Evaluation by Adversary Proceedings", in Ernest House (Ed.), School Evaluation: The Politics and Process. Berkeley: McCutchan Publishing Corporation. 1973; and
Robert L. Wolf, "The Application of Select Legal Concepts to Educational Evaluation," unpublished PhD Dissertation, University of Illinois, 1974.

NINE APPROACHES TO EDUCATIONAL EVALUATION

| APPROACH | PURPOSE | KEY ELEMENTS | PURVIEW EMPHASIZED | PROTAGONISTS (see references) | CASES, EXAMPLES | RISKS | PAYOFFS |
|---|---|---|---|---|---|---|---|
| STUDENT GAIN BY TESTING | To measure student performance and progress | Goal statements; Test score analysis; Discrepancy between goal and actuality | EDUCATIONAL PSYCHOLOGISTS | Ralph Tyler Ben Bloom Jim Popham Mal Provus | STEELE WOMER LINDVALL-COX HUSEN | Oversimplify educ'l aims; Ignore processes | Emphasize, ascertain student progress |
| INSTITUTIONAL SELF-STUDY BY STAFF | To review and increase staff effectiveness | Committee work; Standards set by staff; Discussion; Professionalism | PROFESSORS, TEACHERS | National Study of School Evaluation Dressel | BOERSMA-PLAWECKI KNOLL-BROWN CARPENTER | Alienate some staff; Ignore values of outsiders | Increase staff awareness, sense of responsibility |
| BLUE-RIBBON PANEL | To resolve crises and preserve the institution | Prestigious panel; the visit: Review of existing data & documents | LEADING CITIZENS | James Conant Clark Kerr David Henry | FLEXNER HAVIGHURST HOUSE ET AL PLOWDEN | Postpone action; Over-rely on intuition | Gather best insights, judgment |
| TRANSACTION-OBSERVATION | To provide understanding of activities and values | Educational issues; classroom observation; Case studies; pluralism | CLIENT, AUDIENCE | Lou Smith Parlett-Hamilton Bob Rippey Bob Stake | MacDONALD SMITH-POHLAND PARLETT LUNDGREN | Over-rely on subjective perceptions; Ignore causes | Produce broad picture of program; See conflict in values |
| MANAGEMENT ANALYSIS | To increase rationality in day to day decisions | Lists of options; estimates; Feedback loops; Costs; Efficiency | MANAGERS, ECONOMISTS | Leon Lessinger Dan Stufflebeam Mary Alkin Alan Thomas | KRAFT DOUGHTY-STAKENAS HEMPHILL | Over-value efficiency; Undervalue implicits | Feedback for decision making |
| INSTRUCTIONAL RESEARCH | To generate explanations and tactics of instruction | Controlled conditions, multivariate analysis; Bases for generalization | RESEARCH METHODOLOGISTS | Don Campbell Julian Stanley Mike Scriven Bill Cooley | ANDERSON, R. PELLA ZDEP-JOYCE TABA | Artificial conditions; Ignore the humanistic | New principles of teaching and materials development |
| SOCIAL POLICY ANALYSIS | To aid development of institutional policies | Measures of social conditions and administrative implementation | SOCIOLOGISTS | James Coleman David Cohen Carol Weiss Mosteller-Moynihan | COLEMAN JENCKS LEVITAN TRANKELL | Neglect of educational issues, details | Social choices, constraints clarified |
| GOAL-FREE EVALUATION | To assess effects of programme | Ignore proponent claims, follow check-list | CONSUMERS; ACCOUNTANTS | Michael Scriven | HOUSE-HOGBEN | Over-value documents & record keeping | Data on effect with little co-option |
| ADVERSARY EVALUATION | To resolve a two-option choice | Opposing advocates, cross-examination, the jury | EXPERT; JURISTIC | Tom Owens Murray Levine Bob Wolf | OWENS STAKE-GJERDE REINHARD | Personalistic, superficial, time-bound | Info impact good; Claims put to test |

Of course these descriptive tags are a great over-simplification. The approaches overlap. Different proponents and different users have different styles. Each protagonist recognises one approach is not ideal for all purposes. Any one study may include several approaches. The grid is an over-simplification. It is intended to show some typical, gross differences between contemporary evaluation activities.

28

large programmes using conventional methods summative evaluation might run up to 2 per cent. Smaller programmes, unusual programmes, and highly controversial programmes may need 5 per cent. Formative evaluation can be more expensive, depending on the difficulty of the development problems. In evaluation efforts of the U.S. Experimental Schools it became apparent that agencies could not effectively use substantially more than 5 per cent, perhaps because expectations as to what would be accomplished by the evaluators becomes unrealistic. (The figures in this section are based on the author's own experience as a project director and consultant.)

One good strategy for the commissioning agency is to be explicit as to what kind of observations or what kind of information it needs, and to get the prospective evaluators to indicate how they would do it and what it would cost. They might be encouraged to submit more than one plan, with costs estimated for each. Experienced evaluators will be able to give examples of what other studies have cost - still it is difficult for the commissioners to know how much was accomplished for these expenditures.

The quality of the study is not likely to be related to its cost. The principal concern is to get able persons working on the study. Sometimes they cost very little, sometimes they are not available at any price. The commissioners have to pay the "going rate" for what they want, just as they would for architects, medical doctors or string quartets.

The costs of an evaluation study are not only the expenditure of financial resources, but also largely the use of student, teacher and administrator time. Interference in the programme operations is a substantial cost in some studies, sometimes even causing the evaluation results to be called into question, and encouraging the evaluator to seek unobtrusive methods.(1) A drop in staff morale, community unrest, and increased bureaucratic insensitivity are intangible costs that are sometimes attributed to evaluation programmes.(2) The total costs of an evaluation study are extremely difficult to tally.

There are some reliable expectations as to how financial costs will mount, in addition to the obvious fact that employing more people costs more money. Here are a few:

---

1) See Eugene J. Webb et al., Unobtrusive Measures: Nonreactive Research in the Social Sciences. Chicago: Rand McNally & Company, 1966.
2) See Ernest R. House (Ed.), School Evaluation: The Politics and Process. Berkeley: McCutchan Publishing Corporation, 1973.

1. Sampling a large population is much less expensive than interviewing every teacher or testing every child. However, with small populations, such as that of a single district, the administrative costs of sampling can overcome the savings.
2. The size of sample by specialists in sampling increase costs of data gathering disproportionately above the size needed for answering most evaluation questions.
3. The cost of constructing and validating new instruments or procedures is very high. Existing ones will usually be much cheaper, although perhaps not sufficiently relevant.
4. It is usually a waste of resources to use a standardized instrument for a small number of observations if the instrument is not a part of the clinical tools of the evaluator, the educators or the audience members. Unstandardized observations or questioning are likely to be more informative and less expensive for small operations.
5. The use of computers is necessary in most large-scale data analyses. Computers can save great amounts of personnel time, but their budget lines are often over-funded. Designs for evaluation studies are consistently overly analytic because the computers are so readily available, the costs so easy to justify, and the results so apparently credible. In small studies especially, computer costs should be considered as needing thorough justification.
6. Publication and dissemination costs are regularly much higher than anticipated if there is to be an effective job of circulating the findings.
7. Overhead costs to institutions for use of facilities, libraries, access to experienced personnel, fringe benefits for employees, etc., are as justifiable for evaluation studies as for more conventional research studies.

It would be nice if we could catalogue evaluation costs, showing what findings can be expected to cost, or even what inquiry methods are relatively more costly. But no reliable information of this source can be provided. The commissioner of an evaluation study will have to question experienced researchers and examine budget information from completed studies - and still should expect to rely on guess-work. As with many commodities the prices are very unstable. But given reputable evaluation personnel and with care in writing a good agreement, the commissioner can get his money's worth.

Chapter IV

## NEGOTIATION OF AGREEMENTS TO DO EVALUATION STUDIES

The general purpose of this report is to review the various methods of programme evaluation currently in use in education. A more specific target is the review of the particular responsibility for negotiating an agreement to carry out an evaluation study. In this section the reader will find a listing of issues needing consideration by the commissioners or sponsors of the study and by the prospective evaluators. Three hypothetical conversations between a commissioner and a prospective evaluator have been included to suggest different directions initial conversations may go - depending on the orientation of the evaluation specialist. Comments by experts considering the difficult task of negotiating an agreement to carry out an evaluation study are also included in this section.

### 1. ISSUES FOR CONSIDERATION

It is reasonable to suppose that in addition to the usual consideration of purposes, dates, persons, and costs, the parties working toward an agreement would anticipate the things that could go wrong and take preventive steps, and that they would make real preparations to deal expeditiously with the problems that will occur. That is the pessimistic supposition taken here. "What could go wrong will go wrong" is a useful slogan. The following advice about issues is based not only on theory but on the practice of evaluation in many places, as illustrated in the several case studies in the final section of this report.

A contract can be too specific or not specific enough. If the contract is too specific the evaluator will be unable to respond to unexpected difficulties and opportunities. If the contract is not specific enough the chances of the sponsors getting what they need (and having the grounds for insisting upon it) are reduced. The conversations between commissioners and potential evaluators can also be too specific or not specific enough. If they undertake a detailed technical examination of the programme, the evaluation design, and the possible troubles that might occur, the conversations are likely to de-emphasize the larger policy questions, to disdain the more subtle "unmeasurable" circumstances, and the parties are likely to over-protect themselves with constraints and risk-lowering clauses that could severely limit the opportunity of the evaluation study to be maximally useful. If the conversations are not specific enough (and this is usually the case, sometimes because the commissioner does not want to reveal how little he knows about research methodology and the evaluator does not want to reveal how little he knows about education) then there is little chance for the evaluation study to engage the questions the commissioners need help with and to extend the understandings of the programme in ways that will facilitate decision-making.

Purpose

Perhaps the most important question to be raised, once and again and again, is that of the purposes of the evaluation study. Of course, the purpose of evaluation is to find out what is good and what is bad. In programme evaluation the purpose is to find out the merit and shortcoming of the programme. But the particular questions that concern participants, sponsors, and other constituencies, need more final judgments. They need information, interpretations, recommendations. They need attention to the particulars of the programme. A general review of the merit and shortcoming may fail to address these questions. A hypothesis-testing experimental study may fail to address these questions. Any design might. There may or may not need to be direct attention, for example, to the actual achievements of students. Questions of whether or not the materials are too difficult to read, aimed at the wrong objectives, offensive to parents; questions of whether the teachers are too liberal or conservative, whether or not they know their subject matter; questions of the competence of programme administrators − these are a few of the many imponderables that may be on the minds of programme constituents. The evaluators and commissioners need to examine the range of pertinent questions and to allocate the usually modest resources for evaluation to the few questions that can be given primary attention. Evaluators and commissioners need to consider − not so much the dictionary definition of evaluation, nor the designs of the evaluation methodologist − but what the people involved expect an evaluation study to accomplish.

This is not to say that a good written statement of the purposes or expectations of the evaluation study is not necessary, or that it will assure that the direction of the evaluation is proper. The main thing is for the parties to be satisfied that they know as much as they should about why the evaluation study is being undertaken.

Audiences

It might at first be assumed that the commissioners are the primary audience for the evaluation study, but there usually are others to whom the results will be circulated. Quite often, the commissioners do not expect to learn anything new, and expect that the study will but confirm what they already know. Evaluators need to know who the audiences are so that they may gather data considered most relevant by these audiences, verify observations to meet their standards of credibility, and prepare a presentation of findings in a style that the audiences will find comprehensible and useful.

It is obvious that parents, teachers, students, officials, professors, and others will differ, and differ within their own groups, as to what issues in the programme are most important. Most may be concerned with whether the programme is accomplishing its instructional objectives, but some will not. Some of the time, energy, and funding for the study may need to be spent studying audiences. How the commissioners perceive their audiences is an important first step, and one that needs to be re-checked during the progress of the study.

The evaluators have their audiences too. They want their findings to be shared by research colleagues, they want their good work to be recognised by their superiors, and they want their students or apprentices to learn from the case at hand. Some recognition should be made by the commissioners of these audiences.

Methods of Inquiry

Both parties to the negotiations will have some idea what is appropriate and inappropriate evaluation methodology for the study at hand. There needs to be sufficient discussion of how the study might be carried out so that neither party will feel misled about what is expected by the other. The listing of the nine approaches in the previous section might be used to illustrate some of the techniques desired by either party. If at all possible the prospective evaluator should provide representations of previous work (perhaps a portfolio of instruments, protocols, and reports). The commissioner might show examples of good and poor studies previously done to help the evaluator understand his standards.

It is reasonable to suppose that the evaluator will be the better judge as to which technique is most suitable for answering a particular question, at a particular cost, and at a particular level of credibility. But it should also be recognised that the commissioner will have important ideas as to which techniques have been useful and which have been objectionable in other circumstances.

Because the commissioners feel at a loss, sometimes, to know whether or not a method is reputable, it is not unreasonable for them to appoint a consultant (or for the evaluator to employ an independent reviewer) who will attest to the suitability of methods.

One of the most surprising things to commissioners is the fact that distinguished researchers cannot or will not switch their methods of inquiry. When one chooses an evaluator, one chooses a method of evaluating. Investigators will often redirect their attention to emerging issues and to new opportunities to gather information, but they are less flexible about changing styles of data gathering and analysis. One way they increase their range of methods is to add persons with different styles to the team, or to subcontract a part of the study to another group.

An important part of the methodology is the reporting technique. Evaluators have many different styles of reporting. Experimental psychologists, philosophers, and many "academics" as a group prefer to write a report suitable in style for publication in a scholarly journal. The report may be prestigious, but may be incomprehensible to some important audiences. Some commercial evaluation agencies and local study-groups are prone to make reports that reflect most favourably upon the sponsor. These have public relations value, but are a poor aid to decision-making. Whatever proposal the prospective evaluators make should indicate the style and extent of reporting expected. The commissioners should review this potential commitment carefully.

Confidentiality

Many data used in evaluation studies require confidential handling. Official correspondence, teacher-competence ratings, data on parental income, student reports of misconduct, are some of the more sensitive data, but many individual observations and scores are gathered with the understanding (often implicit) that they will disappear into impersonal summary statistics, their identity remaining undisclosed outside the boundaries of the evaluation project. It used to be that burying information in a computer or in a student's "cumulative file" was considered secure storage, but increased access to computers and files, particularly with new legislation protecting the privacy of individuals, has changed things. The plan for data storage and processing and for circulation of interpretations should be a major provision in the evaluation-study plan.

Certain rules about the release of scores, observations, and quotations will sometimes be needed. It should be stated explicitly which people will have access to the data, the access an individual will have to his own records, how errors may be recognised and corrections made, etc. Any transcripts of tape recordings of meetings, classroom sessions, interviews, etc., may need to be cleared by all who participated. Setting such rules is an integral part of the technology of educational measurement and is part of the ethical responsibility of an evaluator.

One of the most common disagreements that arises between sponsors and evaluators is with the reporting of programme information considered confidential. When this occurs it is likely to be because the evaluator felt obligated to look into matters that were not originally anticipated, then, holding data the programme people recognise as relevant but not appropriate for all audiences, he included it as a report that becomes available to those audiences. If the findings are extremely bad the evaluator may feel a moral obligation to act unilaterally and release them even though the original agreement specified that reports would not be made without the permission of the sponsor or programme personnel. Such situations cannot be dealt with specifically in advance, but it is wise for the commissioner and evaluator to be aware of these possibilities.

## Continuing Negotiations

Even though a formal contract or agreement is signed it is important to consider the arrangements between commissioners and evaluators as requiring monitoring and further negotiating. It often is a mistake to fix a priority or a limit to the study when a better decision can be made after more is understood about the programme and its evaluation. The need for such continuing negotiations should be anticipated and provisions made for modifying the original arrangements.

There are bound to be misunderstandings such as the one mentioned two paragraphs back. How to deal with misunderstanding is no great mystery - one needs contact, communication, empathy, and a willingness to reconsider. But an impasse sometimes is reached. If so, it might have been helpful to have identified, in advance, a group that would act as a "court of appeals". The original negotiations should anticipate the need for subsequent negotiations - not as a sign of fallibility, but as a sign of responsibility.

## 2. CHECKLIST

To assist both the commissioner and the prospective evaluator in covering the many important considerations, the following checklist has been prepared.

Checklist for Negotiating an Agreement to Evaluate an Educational Programme

1. Do the parties to this negotiation know each other? What more do they need to find out? Who wants an evaluation study? Would those not participating (e.g., programme developers, teachers, students) have added an important perspective?

2. What programme is it that is to be evaluated? Whose programme is it? What is its setting? its history? its purposes? its scope? How has it been evaluated before?

3. Why is there to be an evaluation study? What is it expected to produce? What should it accomplish (e.g., recommendations, authoritative judgments, explanations, points of view)?

4. Who are the audiences for the evaluation findings? Will different audiences (e.g., parents, technologists, members of parliament) have different background experience and different information needs?

5. What do the people who are most closely involved with the programme see as its major issues or problems? What issues do other people see? How do all these relate to the major issues facing education elsewhere?

6. What resources are available for the conduct of this study? What cost estimates can be made (e.g., in money, staff time, programme disruption)?

7. What is the work history and working style of the prospective evaluators (i.e., the persons, team, or agency)? Do they have a portfolio of reports and artifacts from completed studies?

8. Why would the evaluators be interested in doing this study? What is there in it for them? Who else would they like to have helping them with it?

9. What will be the primary sources of data? What arrangements would be necessary to gain access to these sources? Are rules of access needed?

10. During the course of the evaluation study, where and how would the data be kept? What would be the rules of access to these data (e.g., to participants, sponsors, newspaper reporters)?

11. What would be a suitable plan for reporting the findings? informal feedback? progress reports? final presentations? Are the evaluators free to publish findings in professional journals? What checks will be made on the effectiveness of the evaluation feedback?

12. How will further arrangements be negotiated after the study begins? What will be the response to unexpected changes in programme? What misunderstandings may arise between the sponsors of the study and the evaluators? How will conflict be resolved?

13. What more needs to be said about the purposes and expectations for the evaluation study?

## 3. HOW ADMINISTRATORS HAVE RESPONDED TO NINE KEY QUESTIONS

How to go about the business of getting an evaluation study started is a different matter in different circumstances. Experienced administrators have different advice to give, partly because they work in different circumstances. Still, there is a substantial agreement among them, as the responses on the following pages indicate.

About 18 administrators were asked to respond, in writing or orally, to the first five questions here. Some raised and answered other questions, and some referred to statements in the professional literature. Included is one statement from an article in Educational Researcher by John Evans of the U.S. Office of Education, stated here as an answer to a key question, though Mr. Evans was not one of the administrators I sought out.

None of the administrators has spoken here for his agency but only as an individual experienced with some aspects of initiating the formal evaluation of educational programmes. What was most apparent from the careful consideration and candid responses given to the questions was an optimism that evaluation studies can facilitate the governance of educational programmes and that good lines of communication between commissioners and evaluators are essential. The answers were made with a quick readiness to share experience. The excerpts on the following pages should help administrators both with large and small experience with evaluation studies to focus on the responsibilities of negotiating productive working arrangements.

The questions started with this heading:

Consider the advice you might pass along to educational officials who are about to commission a large-scale evaluation study. It could be, for example, advice to a West German government agency about to set up an evaluation of special finding of schools having new science programmes, or advice to certain Australian officials about evaluating consultancy services to outback districts. The evaluation is to be done by an outside group, not by staff from the same bureau or ministry.

Making the Evaluation Plans Specific

Question 1: Do you feel that the commissioners should insist on highly specific plans by the evaluators? Which is the greater danger, that the evaluators will focus too early on variables and issues found later not to be important, or that the evaluators will spend so long forming and correcting the design that the results will be incomplete and unsubstantial?

Charles Beltz: Those commissioning a study should make sure that they are clear in their own minds as to what exactly it is that they wish to have evaluated. Often, the negotiations with the evaluators are instrumental in clarifying the thinking of the commissioners. This approach causes a good deal of frustration and argument to both parties, is very time-consuming, and makes unnecessary demands on the evaluators for repeated design modification. How specific any plans for evaluation must be varies from case to case, but if the commissioners have prepared a well thought out brief for the prospective evaluators, the latter are in a much better position to develop an appropriate and acceptable design. Taking this as the basic requirement, there must be sufficient latitude for agreed modifications during the course of the project. Rigid adherence to all of the original design, without amendments arising out of changing circumstances over the time of the project, can make the final outcomes at best incomplete, sometimes irrelevant.

Alphonse Buccino: Plans should be clear, but not necessarily highly specific. By far the greater danger with complex projects is focusing too early on variables and issues which will be found later not to be important.

John Banks: No. The plans for the evaluation should be consistent with the way the experiment has been formulated. The plans should leave room for growing. The danger of too early a focus is more likely, but both are likely.

Stig Obel: It depends on the sort of evaluation the evaluator is up to. A psychometric evaluation should be based on rather specific plans or at least on a model of evaluation with examples from earlier work of the evaluator, showing rather specific variable analysis. In most cases the second danger, that of spending too much time on planning the design, is greater than the first danger. The commissioner should be warned of this danger.

Bryan Dockrell: The keyword is flexibility. That doesn't mean ad hocery or muddling through. It means thinking about the possibilities carefully in advance, specifying possible techniques but keeping the options open for as long as possible. It means too being willing to add additional dimensions to studies as they become relevant. It also means having the courage to acknowledge that data gathered with great care and at great effort is uninformative.

Sally Pancrazio: Partially. Some of the aspects of the plan can be highly specific (time-line, professional staff to be used, available facilities, needs for subcontracting, costs, etc.). Where options in methodology exist, or where actions depend on certain results or findings, the need for such decision points can be specified, as well as the specification of possible options. As an evaluator of proposals and as a reader of final reports, I have not "seen" the latter danger occurring. In fact, the time constraints related to fiscal year appropriations and expenditures prevent the evaluator from spending too much time "forming and correcting the design".

Arieh Lewy: Question 1 should be divided into two portions: first about the specific plan and then about the definition of variables. The preparation of a specific plan does not necessarily require the early definition of the variables. It may be that the plan contains a time schedule which allows for exploratory studies, but which also requires that variables will be defined by a certain date. Moreover, at that time the evaluators should provide "justification" for the selection and definition of the variables. Such justification should be based on the findings of the exploratory investigation.

Generally the plan should be highly specific in a sense that it should contain details about the data areas which should be covered by the study. Examples of such areas are: cognitive behaviours of a higher mental type, transfer of knowledge, interest, co-operation among students, management problems, teachers' and parents' identification with the program. The plan should indicate how these variables should be defined. If they should be based on the results of an exploratory study, how should this study be conducted, how many observations, etc., should be made? The plan should also be specific concerning the sample size, methods of sample selection, and time-table. Such a procedure may avoid both shortcomings mentioned in the question, the focus on variables which are not important and on the attainment of unsubstantial results.

Negotiating a Contract

Question 2: Should the officials and the prospective evaluators meet and negotiate a contract that specifies the design to be used? Is it better to have a long period of negotiations? Does it help such negotiations to refer to previous studies, instruments, reports, and findings?

Bryan Dockrell: Association between the various groups involved in a study should begin early and should be seen as a process of mutual enlightenment. The evaluators will certainly have a job to do in clarifying the limits of the information that they can provide. It is understandably difficult for administrators to realise that a mean score on a test may not convey the information it appears to. The classic example of misunderstanding of this kind is the Stuart and Wells reading survey. The report itself was impeccable. It was nonetheless misunderstood. In these early discussions, reference to previous studies, possible findings, and appropriate instruments would surely play a major part. I do not see these discussions as merely preliminary to a study but an important part of any evaluation. In a study on primary school achievement in one Scottish local authority area, we had a series of meetings with officials followed by the establishment of a steering committee which included representatives of a school system and those in the educational community, the university, colleges of education and ourselves who were primarily contributing expertise to a process of self-examination.

Sally Pancrazio: The negotiation period should not be long. However, I can see that where the proposals do not fit the specifications, and the best proposal needs to be discussed with the submitters in order to bring it "up" to the specifications, that the period of negotiation would require a longer period of time. Most of us want to keep within tight time-lines.

Alphonse Buccino: Officials and evaluators need to extend negotiations over as long a period as necessary to reach a proper understanding.

Arieh Lewy: The inquiry design should definitely be negotiated. Nevertheless the evaluators should insist on adhering to those scientific standards which they feel are relevant to a particular situation. Thus, for example, if instruments should be developed they should not agree to use these instruments without proper validation procedures, even if this may shorten the time needed for the study. In such negotiation, examples of previous studies may be very useful. They help to clarify flaws and merits of other studies and thus they may improve the utility of any new evaluation study.

Constraints on Acess and Publication

Question 3: How important is it for commissioners and evaluators to discuss and make specific agreements on such matters as to who will release information, confidentiality of sources, access to special places? Can you describe any real instance in which failure to discuss such things caused a real problem, or where such an agreement was too constraining?

John Banks: The government feels it owns any information from projects it funds. It expects to control it, even if it anticipates making the information public. It should be the government's responsibility to define cases in which it would feel justified to restrict publication. Two instances of such a problem come to mind, one an economics study and one a study of police records.

Paul Dressel: The evaluator is trying to find out about the worth or value of some enterprise, but he also comes to this task with a set of values. The persons for whom he works and the people whom he evaluates also have a set of values. And very frequently it is the lack of recognition of these values or the clash between the two sets of values or priorities in values which is the source of the difficulty. While I do not think an evaluator needs to insist on a situation in which he can write up and publish everything he finds, or give interviews to the newspapers to insure that all of the difficulties and weaknesses that he locates are broadcast to the public, I think he does need to know whether the people with whom he will be associated will tolerate any critical comment.

Alphonse Buccino: Specific agreements about release of information, and so forth, are absolutely essential. The real instance occurring most often is that certain information may not be made /available/ to evaluators in the absence of such agreements.

Stig Obel: The problem of releasing information is important. The other two aspects are not important. Frequently a published report revealing only part of the picture - from an evaluation of only part of the programme - has been presented as the background for further innovation. In almost every school you can find that reading and writing test results have been used by parents, head teachers, or local authorities to change the programme in the classroom. These tests are not reliable bases for changing the programme in the classroom, and should be used as but one part of a more comprehensive evaluation. An agreement to withhold or release information is not common on this level, but here the dangers are clearly illustrated. In large-scale evaluation studies the problems and dangers are even greater.

Charles Beltz: The issue of publication rights is likely to be a persistent problem because of the different motivations and interests of the parties involved. In the educational area, as distinct from security areas such as defence, it would seem quite possible to come to explicit agreements by which the commissioners undertake to release any progress information and to publish the final report, AS SUBMITTED, and by which the conditions of access to the project's data, subsequent to completion, are clearly determined. Confidentiality of information sources should as a rule be maintained. In fact, it seems most appropriate at completion of the project to either destroy the information permitting identification of sources or deposit it for safe-keeping with the commissioners. The guiding principle should be that the information is supplied for the specific purpose of the project only and not to be used for any other purpose without explicit prior approval of the source.

Arieh Lewy: If no generally accepted standards exist concerning publication procedures, then an agreement should be worked out. On the basis of frictions that have developed in the past over publication of research in Israel, a schedule has been worked out for studies supported by the Ministry of Education. This scheme requires that first the results should be submitted to the commissioners of the study. The commissioners are entitled to criticize the study and to ask further clarification or explanation concerning critical issues. If, following this exchange, the results are stated in a way that satisfies both researchers and commissioners, both sides are free to use the study in any form. If such an agreement is not reached the first publication of the study should include statements in which both sides indicate their views. This practice avoids problems related to publication. Any deviation from this general practice requires previous agreement. Generally it may be a good habit to prespecify the conditions of publication as they are understood by both parties.

Utility of Research

Question 4: How common is it for the evaluators to set up a research study that will be admired by other researchers but not of much use to the commissioning agency?

Ralph Lundgren: Quite common. The agency should obligate the evaluators to be fully conscious of the purposes of the study. Evaluators need to explain the implications of various research approaches.

Charles Beltz: This can cause serious problems where the commissioners are themselves vague in what they want a project to achieve and, by implication, must leave most of the decisions on design, kind of information needed, and outcomes to the evaluators. The central factor of a commissioned study must be its purpose; if it happens also to attract the acclaim of other researchers, that is a happy side-effect, but it should never be its purpose.

Paul Dressel: I have run into a good many evaluators who seem to think that the world was going to be revolutionized as a result of their studies. The evaluator tends to feel that his activities are far more important than they may really be in the life of a large-scale project, and again he may place very great emphasis on certain values which are of much lesser consequence to people who are involved. For evaluation supported out of political deliberations, it is very easy to see why proponents of a particular project are dismayed by anything in the way of a critical evaluation. Political decisions being what they are, any critical comment can be seized upon, blown up, and become the basis for throwing out support of a project - in order to get funds to support something else. One of the greatest problems is matching up the maturity and capability of an evaluator to the persons with whom he works. I have been particularly conscious in this institution over the last ten or fifteen years that, as an institutional researcher and evaluator, I have arrived at the position where I can speak bluntly about the kinds of results found, delineate what ought to be done, and not feel that in the process I was endangering my own status or that of the office. In contrast, I have a report on my desk, which just came in this morning, from a researcher who admits that, because of his concern about critical reactions to certain aspects of this study, he consciously de-emphasized these both in the process of research and again in the process of writing. The net result, I think, is a report which evaded the major issues and which will make very little impact. If I could give any one word of advice to an evaluator as to how to look at the success of his own project, it would be that to find out whether he caused people to think more clearly and deeply rather than whether they changed or replaced the activity.

Arieh Lewy: This seems to be one of the most serious problems in the field of evaluation. The problem becomes even more serious because of the low standards of practice among evaluators. There seems to be a tremendous gap between the competency of top evaluation experts and the general practitioners. The practitioners try to adhere to prefabricated models and designs of study and frequently do not understand the nature of the problem they deal with. Such studies are often admired by their colleagues for adherence to models and for the utilization of complex statistical procedures. The real problem is that in the field of evaluation there are no valid criteria for judging the merits of an evaluation study, and frequently studies are admired without meeting acceptable standards of scientific work. Many evaluation studies published in journals lack even "internal validity". Journal manuscript reviewers judge studies on the finesse of the methodology without examining whether the methodology fits the problem of study.

The Prestige Panel

Question 5: Where can an administrator find guidelines for using - as several of you and your fellow university presidents have - the "blue ribbon" panel to investigate a problem or to evaluate a programme?

David Henry: I can confirm that (James) Conant, (Clark) Kerr and I have "advocated and utilized" blue-ribbon panels, task forces, and study commissions in the evaluation of complex programmes. However, I am at a loss to refer you to any published comment by any of us that would be useful in analyzing the process. I have personally served on four such national groups and feel keenly that they are important, indeed, that they are an essential part of our governance structure in the formulation of public policy. I have not had occasion, however, to put my reactions on paper. Of course, there are many evaluations of individual reports, as you know, and probably somebody has made a general evaluation, but I have not encountered it.

In my seminars on Current Issues and Problems, where I used the reports of national groups as background material, I have introduced the subject about which you write, by noting: 1) the special commission is able to focus on a complex area and bring to its analysis the best in scholarship and current informed opinion; 2) by its nature and the calibre of its people, a commission receives more than ordinary public attention and hence becomes an instrument in public information about problems and issues. Since public policy is or should be the result of extensive public debate, the **commission reports** elevate the conversation beyond mere opinion gathering and place it in the framework of objective analysis and evaluation.

Although some refer slightingly to reports of task forces that "gather dust unnoticed and unread", even a casual study of what really happens to recommendations is quite revealing. For example, all of the recommendations of the Eisenhower Committee on Education Beyond the High School found their way into acceptance within the decade following the report. This is not to say that the committee report created the result. It does suggest, however, that the committee may have helped formulate the nature of the result and its timing. No one, of course, could ever be sure of cause and effect in such an instance. However, the Carnegie Commission on Educational Television resulted directly in the adoption of the Public Television Act of 1968. That tracing is clearly in the record.

Another dimension of the task force is at the state level, by institutions and state governments, and at the local level by municipal governance. It is interesting that some states seem to make greater and more effective use of the blue-ribbon panel approach than others. New York is a study in contrast with Illinois, for example. The New York pattern uses "the blue-ribbon" panel; the Illinois practice favors the representative panel, without so many blue ribbons attached. The former, of course, is always more productive because there are no special interests involved. The latter tends to report the lowest common denominator of consensus among conflictful groups. For that reason, politicians like it.

For Evaluating Innovations

Question 6: What are the essential features of an evaluation of an innovative programme?

John Nisbet: I think we can safely discard as inappropriate the original American model of precisely defined behavioural objectives, measurable outcomes, standardized tests and elaborate statistical analysis. This was summative external evaluation: summative in that it was applied at the end (or sometimes only at the end of the initial stage); external in that it was done by a group separate from the innovators, supposedly neutral but often unsympathetic. Instead, we need a continuous or ongoing evaluation, built into the innovatory programme as an integral part of the team work. This is the model which was developed in the Schools Council 5-13 Project, and the Humanities Curriculum Project. The evaluator is an important member of the team, and he has one of the most difficult jobs to do. He is involved throughout, in the planning (to ensure that evaluation is possible), during the programme (to ensure that relevant records are kept), and at the end of each stage (to provide feedback to the team on their strengths and weaknesses). It is a pattern of formative or responsive evaluation.

Perhaps this may seem to allow too much freedom to the innovators. How do we deal with those who say, "It is clear that there has been a change and we believe that it is a change for the better", or, "We know from our day to day contact that the children are **learning more effectively, and our statement of that conviction is the** only valid evidence"? This is certainly part of the evidence, but the weakness of this style is that it denies to others the right to use their judgment - it withholds evidence. Evaluation is not only a judgment: it also sets out the evidence and reasoning which led to that judgment; and if evaluation is to be accepted as valid, we need to be sure that the evidence reported is a fair sample, and that the reasoning from it is logical, and that alternative interpretations have been considered and disproved. There is no necessity for statistics: recently published evaluations have included case-studies, transcripts, specimens of pupils' work and so on. Evaluation is a form of communication, a sharing of the experience with others. Nowadays, expeditions into high mountains or jungle include a cameraman in the team: the choice of cameraman may be an important factor in winning public sympathy with the aims of the expedition.

> Quoted from "Innovation - Bandwagon or Hearse?" a paper presented at the Frank Tate Memorial Lecture. Melbourne, Australia: Monash University, July 3, 1974.

<u>Generalizing from Studies Elsewhere</u>

Question 7:   Most of the examples of evaluation studies of large-scale educational programmes come from the United States. Some European officials doubt that studying those cases would help them negotiate a contract for evaluation. Why?

Richard Hooper:   I suppose that they could be saying that if you look at America, and the educational culture there, there are some major differences: the whole notion of contracting with anybody to do anything in education, the notion of project proposals, and federal funding, and the Ford Foundation, and professional proposal writers, and ... That is still foreign, foreign as moon landscape, for us in England.

Now you see, not only is it foreign here, it is actively disliked. It is seen as not gentlemanly, not quite on, rather common, a bit vulgar. Education isn't like that. I think in European countries a lot of decisions are made "at the club," amongst gentlemen. The practice - if you like, the democracy - of proposal writing, it doesn't go on here. There is quite a democracy in it, you know; anybody can slap in proposals to the federal government. People here don't know that they could get money from DES (the Department of Education and Science).

So I think that is a major difference. And when you talk about contracting with evaluators, you are immediately assuming that that as a concept is familiar. It isn't. Let's realize that there is not much experience with evaluation studies here.

I think, secondly, that evaluation <u>as a separate activity</u> is totally foreign to most people working in the established parts of education. Someone comes along with a thing called "Evaluation"; and when he starts describing it, they say: "Don't teach your grandmother to suck eggs. We already do that. You are dressing up what we would call common sense with fancy theoretical terms." It is like the response to the sociologist in this country. A sociologist starts talking, and everybody says, "All a sociologist does is point to the blindingly obvious." And evaluation is in the same dangerous area.

Evaluation, as a thing to talk about, is foreign. It is therefore threatening. Especially this evaluation talking about how people make decisions. Our countries are not as open as the U.S. in many ways. The U.S. is much more open, in a sort of investigative journalism, Watergate type of world. That does not go on in Europe.

You want them to study an issue that - they hope - isn't going to be an issue.

## Obstacles to Federal Evaluation Studies

Question 8: In recent years what new problems have arisen in the evaluation of federally supported educational programmes?

John W. Evans: 1. As educational research and evaluation have proliferated, the people and institutions who are the objects of these studies have come under an increasing data collection burden - and are increasingly expressing their resistance to it ...

2. Evaluation studies that involve collecting data on adults are encountering increasing resistance at the interviewee level, particularly among minorities and the poor where it is now not uncommon for respondents to insist that they be paid for their time.

3. The increased sensitivity to evaluation studies - both what they seek to find out and the amount of data they propose to collect - is resulting in a strangling growth of reviews, clearances, and advisory bodies . . . . they threaten to prevent many evaluations from being carried out at all.

4. As protests over evaluation arise, ostensibly over the type and amount of data to be collected, there is likely to be an increased politicization of these protests and their use as weapons in broader disputes between local and federal levels of government.

5. As evaluation activity and policymakers' interest in it have grown, there has also been an increased awareness at the program level that it is necessary to start taking evaluations seriously. This has had the unfortunate effect on some program officers and school administrators of increasing their unwillingness to participate in evaluation studies for fear of what will happen to their programs if the evaluation produces negative findings.

6. Evaluations are increasingly encountering unrealistic expectations on the part of policymakers and legislators with respect to both the speed with which evaluations should be mounted and completed, and the simplicity of the answers which are desired. A demand for evaluation has been created, and it is an increasingly insistent one. Policymakers are beginning to display an irritated impatience with the elaborate trappings of careful design, longitudinal studies, and complex multivariate findings. They want to know whether or not a program is any good and they want to know it yesterday. As unrealistic as these expectations are, evaluators themselves probably must bear some of the blame for them. In their early zeal to have the virtues of evaluation recognized and used, evaluators were almost certainly guilty of overpromising.

7. We are certain to see a lot more public debate of the kind I noted earlier over the validity of evaluation methods and results. An increasingly important and time consuming task for evaluators will be defending the evaluations they carry out and their suitability as a basis for policy decisions.

Quoted from "Evaluating Educational Programs - Are We Getting Anywhere?", Educational Researcher, Vol. 3, No. 8 (September 1974), pp. 7-12.

Advice to Commissioning Agencies

Question 9: What advice would you say is most important for commissioning officials?

Alphonse Buccino: (a) Clarify the purpose to be served by the evaluation and the range of actions to be effected. Get involvement of individuals likely to "use" the evaluation results. (b) Be sure that the program or project to be evaluated is defined with a degree of clarity commensurate with the degree of precision expected of the evaluation. If program outcomes are not well defined, precise measures should not be attempted. (c) Cost of evaluation should be closely related to the potential value of evaluation results. A low-cost survey can, in some instances, yield information as valuable as that coming from a larger effort. (d) Appraise the evaluator's capability for interpretation of data. Data in and of themselves are not very useful in the absence of insightful interpretation.

Bryan Dockrell: Make sure that you understand what the evaluators can provide for you and what they cannot. There is still a touching naivety about the faith of some administrators in evaluation, a naivety which if not fostered is certainly not discouraged by some researchers.

Charles Beltz: (a) Do your homework in preparing a brief for the evaluators. Take the time and make the effort necessary to determine:
- what exactly is to be evaluated;
- what is the purpose of it: increased knowledge or action;
- if action is the purpose, what steps are necessary to prepare for effective implementation following completion of the project;
- what financial resources are likely to be available;
- when are the findings needed, i.e., what are the time constraints;
- what is envisaged in respect of publication, copyrights, confidentiality, etc.

(b) Find a mechanism for a continuous relationship with the evaluators during the whole period of the project. This is a vital aspect of a commissioned project of any size or duration, and I personally favour a steering group or committee convening regularly to:
- maintain contact with the project;
- receive and discuss progress reports;
- act as a forum where either party can air problems, conflicts or new requirements for discussion and settlement;
- advise the evaluators, at their own request or otherwise, on any aspects of the project or relevant new developments or policy decisions.

The composition of such a group would be a point for negotiation but might include, in addition to the two parties, some other persons representing, for example, interest groups or professional expertise.

Stig Obel: Find the right blend of evaluation (psychometric, sociometric, goal-free, and other components) to give a new perspective to the problem.

John Banks: There is a problem selling new evaluation ideas in government. Officials feel competent to deal only with certain ideas, issues, and inquiry methods. There is a tendency to leave the rest to others. But if questions of one kind only go to officials of one kind, e.g., economic questions to economists, then we have a terrible mess on our hands. We need ways of encouraging and protecting agencies for reviewing issues and programmes that extend outside their own specializations.

Frederic Mosher: Consider the particular circumstances. There aren't any general rules yet.

Start far enough ahead to allow yourself to commission a design (or competing designs) which could be worked out by the evaluators in conjunction with the evaluated.

In touchy situations officials and evaluators may want to consider adding a weighty advisory group to endorse or second guess the process and the results. I suspect there is a trade-off between the forcefulness and originality of the work and the safety of numbers. You have to be sensible about the balance.

Plan ahead. Take your time and think out what you want to know and why. Get somebody sensible to help you think about those questions before you plunge in. If the odds are against getting useful answers, don't do it.

Arieh Lewy: Play a simulation game, see what alternative results might be obtained by the evaluative study, and explore the actions to be taken for each different result that might obtain. The evaluation study should be structured in a way that the practical implications of different results will be clear in advance.

The administrators who answered questionnaires or provided statements to permit the foregoing summary were:

John Banks
Department of Education and
  Science
London

Charles Beltz
Assistant Secretary
Department of Education
Australia

Alphonse Buccino
Group Director
Problem Assessment and Special
  Studies
National Science Foundation

W. Bryan Dockrell
Director
Scottish Council for Research
  in Education

Paul L. Dressel
Assistant Provost for
  Institutional Research
Michigan State University

John W. Evans
Office of Planning, Budgeting
  and Evaluation
U.S. Office of Education

David D. Henry
President Emeritus
University of Illinois

Richard Hooper, Director
National Development Programme in
  Computer Assisted Learning
London

Arieh Lewy
Ministry of Education
  and Culture
Israel

Ralph Lundgren
Eli Lilly Foundation
Indianapolis,
Indiana

Frederick A. Mosher
Program Officer
Carnegie Corporation
  of New York

John Nisbet, Head of Department
  of Education
University of Aberdeen
Scotland

Stig Obel
Inspector of Education
Ministry of Education
Copenhagen

Sally F. Pamcrazio, Director
Department of Research and
  Statistics
Illinois Department of Education

## 4. HOW RESEARCHERS HAVE RESPONDED TO SEVEN KEY QUESTIONS

There are differences among researchers, as there are in any group, as to the best methods for getting the job done. This pertains, as well, to the job of commissioning an evaluation study. Some researchers prefer very formal negotiations, with a careful specification of the purpose, the procedures, and the responsibilities. Some prefer a minimum of specific procedural commitments, but well-defined methods for monitoring developments and resolving disagreements. And some prefer the least acknowledgment that there are expectations and obligations on both sides.

Many things happen in the course of a programme evaluation study that change the nature of the programme and its evaluation. Some anticipation of these changes is necessary. Some discussion of them between commissioner and evaluator is recommended by almost all experienced parties. But there is disagreement as to how many potential calamities should be considered, and more disagreement as to how formally they should be recognised in any contract or agreement made. Both parties need protection when things go awry. It is best to get that protection spelled out early. But most problems cannot be adequately anticipated, and the very discussion of potential problems is likely to get the focus of the evaluation shifted, and the range of issues narrowed, so that the evaluation may be dealing with them, sometimes properly so, and sometimes overly so. The overworking of these possibilities may cause the purposes of the evaluation to become limited to the superficial things less likely to become troublesome, and the issues may not be those that really concern the audiences.

In order to identify how researchers respond to this sort of situation, a small group of them were asked seven questions. From the lengthy and thoughtful answers they sent in the statements on the following were selected.

Choosing the Methods of Inquiry

Question 1:  The researcher feels that sometimes a sponsor prefers a form of investigation that is not suitable for the issues at hand. Should the evaluator be guaranteed the freedom to choose the methods of inquiry to be used? Is this an important issue?

David Hamilton: Yes - an important issue. I don't think the evaluator should be guaranteed the freedom any more than the sponsor should be guaranteed the right to determine the research (Who are the sponsors anyway? The Ford Foundation? The shareholders? The workers? Or those who buy the cars?). I think that the sponsors have the right to specify the problems they would like addressed, then it's up to them and the evaluator to decided upon the means.

Dan Stufflebeam: This obviously is an important issue but my answer is no. I think that any evaluation design is a collection of decisions concerning many things including audiences, questions to be addressed, authorship of reports, editorial license, delivery schedule of evaluation products, schedule of payments, access to personnel and program data, right of rebuttal, and so forth. These decisions can greatly affect the welfare of programs and personnel as well as the quality and utility of the evaluation work performed. Hence I think that these items should be considered negotiable and that representatives of the groups to be involved in and affected by the evaluation should negotiate the items in advance of conducting the study and that the resultant contract should serve as a guide for the study. Of course, the contract should include a clause for allowing review and renegotiation. Further, any evaluator who cannot reach acceptable agreements with clients can refuse to enter into an evaluation relationship or if already employed by the agency, can quit. Both such events have occurred several times in the past, but probably not often enough.

Thomas Owens: The choice of methods of inquiry is an issue that should be settled by negotiation between the evaluation contractor and the sponsoring agency. In some cases involving competitive bid, the evaluator's proposed choice of methodology may be a critical factor in deciding which evaluation agency is selected. The agency preparing a RFP (Request for Proposal) may also have strong preferences for a particular methodology and if so, should specify them in the RFP. Obviously some methodologies are less appropriate than others for answering certain key questions. A sophisticated government bureau should probably know in advance the key questions it wants the evaluation to answer and which methodologies would or would not be adequate to answer these questions. Also the funding agency may need to express any constraints that would rule out certain methods of inquiry for technical, political or financial reasons.

Marvin Alkin: I think the evaluator has to have the final say regarding methodologies. The agency has to find its protection in on-time submission of a technical complete and correct report directed towards decision concerns prespecified.

Alan Thomas: The evaluator should have considerable latitude in selecting the method to be used. In extreme cases he should refuse to undertake a task if he is constrained to use methods he feels are inappropriate.

Karl Frey and Manfred Lang: Some points have to be discussed and decided in co-operation with the sponsor and will partially influence the choice of methods.

In general the evaluator should have the freedom to choose among possible alternatives. He knows the pros and cons and validity of methods.

## "Piggy-backing" Basic Research

Question 2: The evaluator sometimes says that some of his research effort must go into the basic questions of education. Should the evaluator ask for assurance that some of the effort in each study be devoted to basic research? Is this an important issue?

Ernest House: The evaluator *may* ask for some resources for basic research but the sponsor is under no obligation to provide them - and should not do so most of the time. Becoming fixated on research issues is likely to lure the evaluator from the particular focus of his task - the particularities and peculiarities of the project itself.

Robert Rippey: The issue is important. However, I think that it is more important to get competent, inquiry-oriented evaluators functioning than it is to impose specific basic research expectations on a particular project. In some instances, it may be more important to implement a promising idea and study it once implemented than to preordain basic research objectives on an entity which may never fly. Research can often appear threatening prospectively. Perhaps better research can be done once rapport is developed, and the researcher has a more intimate understanding of what he is studying, than he might in advance. I am currently exploring a fascinating research question using some data I would not have had access to if I had demanded research assurances in advance of my involvement. Research, yes. Assurances - dysfunctional at times.

Malcolm Parlett: It depends on personal preference. Personally, I think that the proper study of education proceeds through studies of real life educational phenomena and problems encountered by educators. To do good applied work inevitably means raising basic questions of education. In other words, it is a false dichotomy.

Murray Levine: It is and is not an important issue. It is important from the perspective of the university based researcher, who needs to have research pay off in a career sense. It is also important in that available funds ought to be used in the most efficient manner, and if a basic question can be posed while contributing to the evaluation, so much the better. The key is the word basic. If basic means using the evaluation situation to test some academic theory, where the primary interest is in the variables of the theory, then I would say the inclusion of such matters is secondary from the point of view of the sponsor of the research. However, if some really critical question can be readily incorporated into the research design, and have payoff for the sponsor, then it should be done. For example, Peter Bryant makes a simple suggestion in his new book that the teaching of reading to young children might be facilitated by the simple expedient of putting a red line down the left side of the page to provide a frame of reference for left right spatial orientation in young children. The left right orientation is poorly developed. That sort of idea could be tested readily, it has practical implications, and it could be incorporated into an evaluation design with very little cost. That kind of thing should be done wherever feasible.

Ralph Tyler: An evaluation organization should have a research program to which each evaluation effort should make some contribution.

Alan Thomas: I believe the researcher has the right and the responsibility to ensure that some of his effort is devoted to the advancement of knowledge. An important issue.

Publishing in Journals

Question 3: The evaluator sometimes wants to publish results in a professional journal. Should there be any restrictions on what he might publish there?

David Cohen: I can see none a priori, though agencies ought to have the right to reply in the same issue of the journal.

Julian Stanley: It seems to me that usually an evaluator should be free to publish in professional places articles or even books based on his evaluation, after a report of it is submitted and discussed.

Murray Levine: I think the only restrictions should be those consistent with confidentiality. I have on several occasions made an agreement with those involved that I would submit what I write for prior review with the understanding that I would control what was included and what was said. I did agree to include in the body of the work itself disagreements of interpretation, or statements of explanation so the party affected would have his or her interests represented. I have found that an effective tactic in relation to evaluation reports, and in relation to publication of a report.

Ralph Tyler: Generally, knowledge grows from publications. The evaluation organization should clarify in its contract what freedom of publication is appropriate.

Malcolm Parlett: This is obviously something that can be discussed in advance, though the evaluator will often have to put up with the sponsor saying, "let's wait and see, until we have had a look at what you are going to write". My own feeling here is that the evaluator does not have to take the assignment if he/she does not like the conditions imposed. On the other hand, he/she can seek to persuade the sponsor to provide permission for publication - especially on the grounds that wider communication of educational experiences is necessary.

Robert Rippey: I can work with some restrictions and not others. The conditions should be clearly stated. It is the evaluator's responsibility to draw up the specifications.

Thomas Owens: If the professional journal article is based upon data that have not become public domain I feel it is appropriate for the evaluator to get approval from the contracting agency for such publishing. In some cases the contracting agency may wish to release certain data prior to allowing them to be published privately by the evaluator.

Ernest House: There should be restrictions on journal articles but these restrictions should be negotiated in advance. In particular, the sponsor should have no right to censor information in the report unless the agreed-upon procedures call for such editing. For the sponsor to be the final arbiter of what shall see the light of day is not healthy.

Malcolm Provus: Yes. Client confidentiality - within the terms of his contract - comes first.

Disclosing Malfeasance

Question 4: The evaluator sometimes finds something that he feels must be reported to higher authority or to the public, even though his contract calls for confidential treatment of information. Should the evaluator ask for assurance that he can follow his conscience in such instances?

Wynne Harlen: Following one's conscience is probably independent of contracts, i.e., one would risk breaking a contract if an issue was sufficiently important. However, to avoid confrontation it would be best if the evaluator were formally given the right of decision as to whether information which others prefer to be kept confidential should be reported.

Julian Stanley: This is a tricky matter and can be answered only "It all depends . . ." Presumably, his evaluation should not be kept secret or heavily edited, but in most instances it would not seem desirable for the evaluator to go to news media or others to spring his findings before they are reported to the sponsor. He should, however, have assurances that the report will be made public within a reasonable length of time after it is submitted. It seems to me that secret evaluations by professionals are seldom justified.

Malcolm Parlett: This possibility certainly has to be addressed in advance. Often it may be hypothetical, but possibilities such as these should certainly be paraded early in the game. The evaluator, in my view, has to make it clear that he/she has to exercise his/her very best judgment in questions of ethical responsibility. There is a 'grey area' where it is impossible to anticipate each and every moral conundrum, and this has to be acknowledged openly at the outset. Obviously any breaking of the confidentiality 'contract' would have to be in extreme circumstances, and examples of what these might be could be raised by the evaluator in the preliminary discussion.

Dan Stufflebeam: The answer to this one depends on the prior contract that was negotiated and on provisions for renegotiation as well as basic moral questions that might be involved once the findings are known. Generally I prefer the case where the contract gives authority to the evaluator to release his report whether or not the report is endorsed or appreciated by the sponsor. In this case, of course, there is no problem, at least not the kind you are referring to in proceeding to release the information to the public. In another case where the evaluator thinks he ought to release the information because of political pressure, because of possibility for pervasive impact, etc., I believe the evaluator should not be the sole decision maker if he has previously agreed to limit his report to certain defined audiences. Instead, I think he must reopen the negotiation of the contract and seek to reach agreements with the other parties concerning whether the information should be released and then should honor such agreements. Of course, there are times when questions of basic morality such as emerged in the Watergate mess present themselves. Then I think the evaluator must do what he believes, based on his own conscience, must be done for the welfare of society and in consideration of the interests of the persons to be affected by the release.

Ralph Tyler: No one individual's conscience should be accepted as valid. The way in which information will be treated should be part of the contract.

## Attention to Evaluation Findings

Question 5: The evaluator is sometimes discouraged by the little attention given his findings. Should the evaluator ask for assurance that his words will be heeded?

Julian Stanley: Realistically, would <u>asking</u> do any good? He can query the agency officials carefully before he contracts with them, but they may, nevertheless, try to bury or ignore his findings.

Dan Stufflebeam: This is a very tough question, highlighting one of the most important problems evaluators have. By and large I think our methodology is poor for communicating with audiences, for working with audiences toward the application of information. We have too often felt that our work was done once we had prepared a 300-page report and sent it to the sponsoring agent. To provide some minor improvement, I recently proposed a new definition of evaluation that would, I think, place more attention on the communication process. The definition I proposed is:

Evaluation is the process of delineating, obtaining, and applying descriptive and judgmental information for decision making and accountability.

Whereas the "obtaining" step is intended to be the technical one of collecting, organizing, and analyzing information, the "delineating" and "applying" steps are interface steps. Of course clients, evaluators, and other interested parties must interface early in the study and periodically throughout to effect and evolve the agreements that guide the study. As to the applying step, the evaluator has the difficult job of providing information through writing and disseminating reports, through face-to-face meetings, through dissemination of findings through the public media, etc. At the same time the audiences and the client particularly must utilize the information (or ignore it) in regard to decision making, accountability, public relations, and so forth. My feeling is that we have to do a great deal more than we have done to incorporate communication theory and change theory into the methodology of evaluation. Evaluation, after all, essentially is a change process. If it is to produce improvements or changes of any kind, it seems reasonable that the well-known change principle of involvement of those whose behavior is to be affected ought to be incorporated into our plans for applying evaluative information to the larger change process. I guess I would say that this problem area is probably the number one priority item that evaluators ought to be attending to.

Robert Stake: The evaluator may own his words but he does not own their meaning. The meanings the reader gives - based often on more relevant experience - are more important than those the evaluator gives. The evaluator should not presume he knows best how much his words are worth.

David Hamilton: If the evaluator takes care to address the pertinent questions, then there is a much greater chance that his findings will be attended to. To my mind the choice of questions to focus upon is the most critical part of the evaluator's job.

Wynne Harlen: An evaluator has no more right, purely as a right, to have his words heeded than anyone else. He must present his findings so that their claim to be heeded is self-evident.

Abuse of Evaluation Findings

Question 6: The evaluator sometimes finds that his findings are used as if they supported claims that they do not. Should the evaluator ask for assurance that this will not happen?

Alan Thomas: Yes. However, it often happens that persons over whom he has no control will misinterpret his results.

Julian Stanley: From his sponsors, yes - and if they do so anyway he should attempt to rebut their inaccurate claims. I do not see how one can prevent the press from distorting its reports of evaluations, and it is difficult to say to what extent the evaluator himself should try to correct misimpressions created by the press. That might require much of his (unreimbursed) time and effort, without sufficient professional payoff.

Ralph Tyler: It is not legally possible to ask in advance, but he can assure the sponsor that misinterpretations will be made public if they occur.

Malcolm Parlett: This is difficult. If the evaluator begins to raise questions like this, he/she is unlikely to win trust and confidence. I do not think there is much that can be done over this phenomenon.

Ernest House: The evaluator must take care that his report is not censored, edited, or changed in substance without his knowledge. But like a poet, he cannot determine all interpretations and all uses to which his work will be put. He may wish to refute some interpretations publicly and he may be wrong in his own interpretation. Certainly though, he cannot wash his hands of all responsibility. He may wish to guard against his work being used in particularly unsavory ways, such as being used to injure people.

Thomas Owens: The abuse referred to in this question does, of course, occur from time to time but prior assurance that this will not happen may have little effect in preventing it. I do not feel that a formal assurance should be requested. It assumes that the contracting agency is unprofessional.

Donald Campbell: No! Freedom of information applies to sponsor's freedom too. But the evaluator should demand the right to publicize his interpretation to the same audiences.

Karl Frey and Manfred Lang: Misuse of results can only be regretted by those who didn't consider the consequences of results in a political system of norms. A reassurance is meaningless and no substitute for a thought in advance about possible means to compensate or suppress misleading interpretations.

The evaluator should make sure that his results and data are not misused. This can be done by explicating his design hypotheses, samples, methods of assessment and analysis and by giving an **unambiguous interpretation. More than this reassurance is not possible.**

Last Minute Advice to Evaluators
---

Question 7: If you were to advise evaluators going into negotiations of their first agreement to conduct an evaluation study, what would you say to them?

Thomas Owens: Lots of luck! Investigate the government bureau's relationship with previous evaluators. Determine _why_ they want an evaluation done. Find out the constraints being placed on the evaluation. Establish in advance the person(s) to whom the evaluator would be responsible and the procedures to be followed in modifying the contract if necessary.

David Hamilton: (1) The future career of the evaluation rests on the outcomes of these negotiations. (2) They should not be hurried - keep talking/asking. (3) The negotiations are just the first part of an ongoing dialogue. If the scene is set properly, the actors will be better able to play their parts. (4) Do not make promises which you know to be unattainable. Focus on the possible. (5) Keep thinking and rethinking.

Robert Rippey: (1) Make certain your agreement touches all the six previous questions. Make sure it is understood by all. (2) Make certain everyone you will contact and everyone who is likely to hear about your activity knows about you, what your intents are, and how to communicate with you. Also make sure you take some initiative for touching base with them. (3) Realize that evaluation and change can be threatening. Allow ample opportunities for feedback to be expressed by all participating. (4) Organize your work carefully.

Have clear statements of procedures at the outset written so they are understood. Assign clear responsibilities. Set time deadlines. Describe procedures, methodology, instrumentation, and analysis early. (5) Make certain that you do not overlook the degree to which implementation takes place and the effect which implementation has on the feelings of all affected. (6) Spend a lot of time finding out what is wanted - what the purpose of the evaluation is and what will be helpful to the project. (7) Do not be aloof. Consider evaluation as part of the "treatment". For replication, evaluation procedures should be replicated as well as treatment. That is, any description of treatment should include a description of the evaluation. Evaluation does not interact with treatment - it *is* treatment. If treatment is "going to hell" and you know why, tell someone. Give advice. A lot of times the evaluator simply knows more than anyone else in a program he is evaluating, at least about the dysfunctional aspect he has uncovered.

Ernest House: The evaluator works with the sponsor. He is not superior to him nor is he servile because the sponsor is paying the fee. The evaluator has a responsibility to the sponsor to be as fair and as helpful as he can be. He also has an obligation to the ultimate consumers, whether they be teachers, parents, or children, to be honest in his work and careful in its dissemination, so they will come to no harm. This dual obligation imposes an independence on the evaluator which must be newly negotiated within each setting. The evaluator must assume the final responsibility for the integrity of his work.

Karl Frey and Manfred Lang: If an evaluator has the difficulties formulated in these seven questions, he should at first check his attitudes toward science. Does he accept only scientific truth or, in addition, normative truths. Does he believe truth finds its way without help or truth is dependent on the cognitive and emotional structure (Bewusstsein) of humans and of the material conditions in a society. If he accepts normative truths as a reality he should act politically, i.e. try to find and co-operate with people in agreement with his ideas, make personnel policy, know the rules of an institution and his organization and its maintenance.

Julian Stanley: Be very careful and thoughtful. Take your time. Consult with trusted colleagues. Get the full agreement into writing and consider that fully. Charge as high a price as feasible so that your report is more likely to be considered valuable. Be sure that you will be compensated well for all your efforts, including the final "clean-up". Do not do a free feasibility or pilot or preliminary study. Get paid for it too, because if you are a true professional and insist on strong safeguards, you stand an excellent chance of not getting the contract.

Malcolm Parlett: These negotiations are important. Don't rush them, and don't rush into a commitment to do the study. Find out why the study is being done; why they have asked you to do it. Find out as much as possible about the background circumstances, their expectations, and the freedom that they intend to give you. Find out whether you are going to have a free hand, or if not, how your autonomy is being restricted. Try to get as much in writing as possible, perhaps summarising what you see as the decisions made, and agreements reached, writing them up in memorandum form. Send this memorandum to them and ask them whether they agree with what it contains. There will be some areas, grey areas, where nobody can tell in advance what is likely to transpire; new difficulties may arise, and ethical problems present themselves. These cannot be foretold in detail, but the likelihood of their occurring can be adjudicated, and your likely response to various hypothetical circumstances can be speculated about. Try and build an understanding relationship with them, in such a way that you can come back and negotiate with them further, in a climate of mutual trust and forebearance. Understand that they have a job to get done, and that they will not be able to see all the research difficulties nor the pressures upon the evaluative researcher, themselves. Try and make clear the types of professional dilemma that can arise, the hesitancies that you have, etc. Try and see their point of view as much as possible; also try to get them to see yours. If you feel uncomfortable with the arrangements, and cannot get them clarified to your satisfaction, or you don't trust the individuals to keep their side of the informal bargains made, think twice before finally taking on the assignment. If things foul up, and you are pitched headlong into a personal/political/moral morass, the attraction and enjoyment of doing the study will be quickly dissipated. If you are flat broke, out of work, and desperately need to do the study, you may need to take it on while still having reservations. However, do the utmost possible to ensure that there are not contradictory perceptions of what you are going to do, and that the problems about 'who talks to whom', when is feedback going to come", etc. are discussed in advance of their looming up in unexpected and threatening ways. At the same time, don't make the contract so rigid that it cannot be renegotiated or recast as the study progresses. Build in some escape clauses if you discover that you cannot do the job that you said you could. Don't take on more than you can do - don't get carried away. Above all, understand that those evaluated, those that you are responsible to, or those involved, are working for something that they believe in, or that they have responsibility for. You have a license to enter into their world. Don't treat them in any way that you would not like yourself to be treated, by an outside evaluator coming into your world.

The researchers who answered questionnaires to permit this summary were:

Marvin Alkin
Center for the Study
   of Evaluation
University of California
Los Angeles, California

Donald Campbell
Department of Psychology
Northwestern University

David Cohen
Center for Educational
   Policy Research
Harvard University

Karl Frey and Manfred Lang
Institut für die Padagogik der
   Naturwissenschaften
Universitat Kiel

David Hamilton
Department of Education
University of Glasgow

Wynne Harlen
Progress in Learning Science
University of Reading

Ernest House
Center for Instructional Research
   and Curriculum Evaluation
University of Illinois

Murray Levine
Department of Psychology
State University of New York
Buffalo, New York

Thomas Owens
Northwest Regional Educational
   Laboratory
Portland, Oregon

Malcolm Parlett
Nuffield Foundation
London, England

Malcolm Provus
Evaluation Research Center
University of Virginia

Robert Rippey
Office of Research
   in Health Education
University of Connecticut

Robert Stake
Center for Instructional Research
   and Curriculum Evaluation
University of Illinois

Julian Stanley
Study of Mathematically
   Precocious Youth
John Hopkins University

Dan Stufflebeam
Center for Evaluation
Western Michigan University

Alan Thomas
Department of Education
University of Chicago

Ralph Tyler
Center for Advanced Study
Palo Alto
California

## 5. THREE HYPOTHETICAL CONVERSATIONS

The following dialogues illustrate the difficulties a commissioner and a prospective evaluator have in getting acquainted with what the other person needs and expects. Three were written rather than one to show how evaluators of different persuasions respond. There is obviously common concern among these three evaluators, but clear differences as well.

The first evaluator stresses the need for maximum attention to results that are directly related to the instruction. The second evaluator stresses finding out the problems that most concern the people involved in this particular programme. The third evaluator stresses the need to remain independent of sponsors and programme personnel. These three evaluators represent the approaches in the grid in Section III-2 that were called Student Gain by Testing, Transaction-Observation, and Goal-Free Evaluation Approaches. It is reasonable to expect that the three contracts they would write would be quite different, both in terms of what they would promise and in terms of the safeguards they would set forth.

Following the second dialogue is a collection of responses from eight administrators who were in a position to commission such a large-scale evaluation study. These responses were made after they were invited to consider the concerns of the commissioner in the second dialogue and to note the uniqueness or generality of the situation.

### A conversation between a person who will commission an evaluation study and an evaluation specialist favouring a consequence orientation

C: Thanks for taking the time to see me today. I suspect that your teaching schedule at the University keeps you hopping, but I've been told that you occasionally carry out educational evaluations.

E: That's true, my normal teaching load here at the University is pretty heavy, but this quarter is about over. Besides, I am working now with a small group of graduate students in an evaluation seminar, and when I mentioned the possibility of evaluating your district's project in Reality-Rooted Reading they became really interested.

C: You mean you might use students in carrying out an evaluation?

E: It's really good experience for them, and they often can make excellent contributions to the evaluation itself. Of course, one must be careful not to exploit students in such situations. Too many of my colleagues view graduate students as a somewhat advanced form of migrant workers.

C: Well, did you have a chance to read the write-up I sent you of our new Reality-Rooted Reading programme? We think it holds great promise as a way to get poor readers more involved in developing their reading skills.

E: I did read the document, and you may be correct. There are certainly a number of positive features in the programme. I must confess, though, that I was disturbed by the apparent lack of replicability in the programme itself. It sounds more like a six ring circus than anything which, if it does work, could be used again in the future. If you're going to the trouble of evaluating this intervention, I assume that you're contemplating its use in the future. Interventions that are not at least somewhat replicable can't really be employed very well in the future. Is your Reality-Rooted Reading programme going to be essentially reproducible?

C: I'm glad you brought that up. The planning committee which has been working out the programme's details became aware of that problem a few weeks ago. They're in the process of devising instructional guides which will substantially increase the replicability of the programme.

E: I just hope the planning committee itself is rooted in reality.

C: Well, what about the evaluation? Will you take it on? Our district school board is demanding formal evaluations of all new programmes such as this one, so we can't really get under way until the responsibility for evaluation has been assigned.

E: I'll need to get some questions answered first.

C: Fire away.

E: What's the purpose of the evaluation? In other words what's going to happen as a consequence of the evaluation? Unless the evaluation is going to make a genuine difference in the nature of the instructional programme, we wouldn't want to muck with it. Too many of us here at the University have experienced the frustrations of carrying out research studies whose only purpose seemed to be that of widening the bindings of research journals. Unless an evaluation satisfies the "so what?" criterion, I'm sure we wouldn't be interested.

C: Well, the district superintendent has indicated that the continuation of the new programme will be <u>totally</u> dependent upon the results of its evaluation. That satisfy you?

E: Sure does. Now, there was a bit of rhetoric in your programme description about appraising the programme in terms of the "uniqueness of its innovative features". Does that imply you're more concerned with evaluating the procedural aspects of the programme than with evaluating the results yielded by those procedures? This is a particularly important issue for me.

C: Well, we are very proud of the programme's new features. What are you getting at?

E: There are too many educators who are so caught up with the raptures of an instructional innovation that they are almost oblivious of its effects on learners. And that, after all, is why we're in the game. Our instructional interventions should help learners. I want to be sure that, although we will consider the procedures employed during the programme, the main emphasis of the evaluation will focus on the consequences of that programme's use.

C: Oh, we'd be perfectly agreeable to that. After all, you people are the experts. Besides, I guess I share your point of view.

E: I also noted an almost exclusive preoccupation with cognitive, that is, intellectual outcomes of the programme. Your people seemed to be concerned only about the skills of reading. Aren't you also worried about pupils' attitudes toward reading?

C: Of course, but you can't assess that kind of stuff can you? I thought the affective domain was off-limits for the kinds of evaluators who, as you apparently are, are concerned with evidence.

E: It's tough to do, but there are some reasonably good ways of getting evidence regarding learners' affect toward an instructional programme. We'd want to use them.

C: How about tests? Will you have to build lots of new ones?

E: My guess is that we will have to devise some new measures. The standardized teaching tests your district now uses will be worthless for this kind of an evaluation. We'll need to see if there are any available criterion-referenced tests which we can use or adapt.

C: Do you people always have to use tests?

E: No, **but it is** important to get sufficient evidence regarding a programme's effects so that we are in a better position to appraise its consequences than merely by intuiting those consequences.

C: You'll still have to make judgments, won't you?

E: Certainly, but judgments based on evidence tend to be better than judgments made without it. Properly devised measuring devices can often be helpful in detecting a programme's effects, both those that were intended as well as any unanticipated effects.

C: How come I haven't heard you say "instructional objectives" once during our conversation? I thought you folks were all strung out on behavioural objectives.

E: Well, clearly stated instructional objectives represent a useful way of describing a programme's intended effects. But the <u>effects</u> of the programme are what we want to attend to, not just the educator's utterances about what was supposed to happen. Consequence-oriented educational evaluators can function effectively even without behavioural objectives.

C: Amazing!

E: There are a couple of other areas we have to get into. I hope you're sincere in wanting to contrast the new programme with alternative ways that the money it's costing might be spent.

C: Absolutely.

E: And, finally, the matter of evaluator independence. Will we have the right to release the results of our evaluation to all relevant decision-makers involved in this project, including the public?

C: You think that's important to get clarified now?

E: It might head off some sticky problems later. We'd like that kind of independence.

C: I think it can be assured. I'll want to check it out with my division chief, however;

E: There's also a related kind of independence I want to discuss. Unlike some of the independent evaluation firms that have sprung up in the past few years, we really aren't in the evaluation business on a full-time basis, hence in a sense we don't need your district's repeat business. Therefore, we'll be inclined to call our shots openly, even if it means that the programme is evaluated adversely.

C: That's related to your earlier point about independence in reporting the evaluation's results.

E: You bet.

C: Okay, we're willing to play by the rules. I hope it turns out positively though.

E: So do I. Our kids could surely do with a bit of help in their reading programme.

C: Well, what next?

E: Why don't I and some of my students whip up a detailed plan of how we want to do the evaluation and fire it off to you by mail, say, in two weeks.

C: Fine. If we have any problems with it, we can get back to you. All right?

E: Sure.

C: We haven't talked about money yet. How much will this thing cost?

E: We'll include a budget with our evaluation plan. But, because university professors are so handsomely rewarded by their own institutions, I'm sure the amount will be a pittance, perhaps a used chalkboard eraser or two.

C: You guys do live in an invory tower, don't you?

E: Didn't you take the elevator on the way up?

## A conversation between a person who will commission an evaluation study and an evaluation specialist favouring a responsive approach

C: As I said in my letter I have asked you to stop by because we need an evaluator for our National Experimental Teaching Programme. You have been recommended very highly. But I know you are very busy.

E: I was pleased to come in. The new Programme is based on some interesting ideas and I hope that many teachers will benefit from your work. Whether or not I personally can and should be involved remains to be seen. Let's not rule out the possibility. There might be reasons for me to set aside other obligations to be of help here.

C: Excellent. Did you have a chance to look over the programme materials I sent you?

E: Yes, and by coincidence, I talked with one of your field supervisors, Mrs. Bates. We met at a party last week. She is quite enthusiastic about the plans for group problem-solving activities.

C: That is one thing we need evaluation help with. What kind of instruments are available to assess problem-solving? Given the budget we have, should we try to develop our own tests?

E: Perhaps so. It is too early for me to tell. I do not know enough about the situation. One thing I like to do is to get quite familiar with the teaching and learning situations, and with what other people want to know, before choosing tests or developing new ones. Sometimes it turns out that we cannot afford or cannot expect to get useful information from student performance measures.

C: But surely we shall need to provide some kind of proof that the students are learning more, or are understanding better, than they did before! Otherwise how can we prove the change is worthwhile? We do have obligations to evaluate this programme.

E: Perhaps you should tell me a little about those obligations.

C: Yes. Well, as you know, we are under some pressure from the Secretary (of Health, Education and Welfare), from Members of Congress, and the newspapers. They have been calling for a documentation of "results".

But just as important, we in this office want to know what our programme is accomplishing. We feel we cannot make the best decisions on the amount of feedback we have been getting.

E: Are there other audiences for information about the National Experimental Teaching Programme?

C: We expect others to be interested.

E: Is it reasonable to conclude that these different "audiences" will differ in what they consider important questions, and perhaps even what they would consider credible evidence?

C: Yes, the researchers will want rigor, the politicians will want evidence that the costs can be reduced, and the parents of students will want to know it helps their children on the College Board Examinations. I think they would agree that it takes a person of your expertise to do the evaluation.

E: And I will look to them, and other important constituencies, teachers and taxpayers, for example, to help identify pressing concerns and to choose kinds of evidence to gather.

C: Do you anticipate we are going to have trouble?

E: Of course, I anticipate some problems in the programme. I think the evaluator should check out the concerns that key people have.

C: I think we must try to avoid personalities and stick to objective data.

E: Yes, I agree. And shouldn't we find out which data will be considered relevant to people who care about this programme. And some of the most important facts may be facts about the problems people are having with the programme. Sometimes it does get personal.

C: The personal problems are not our business. It is important to stick to the impersonal, the "hard-headed" questions, like "How much is it costing?" and "How much are the students learning?"

E: To answer those questions effectively I believe we must study the programme, and the communities, and the decision-makers who will get our information. I want any evaluation study I work on to be useful. And I do not know ahead of time that the cost and achievement information I could gather would be useful.

C: I think we know what the funding agencies want: information on cost and effect.

E: We could give them simple statements of cost, and ignore such costs as extra work, lower morale, and opportunity costs. We could give them gain scores on tests, and ignore what the tests do not measure. We know that cost and effect information is often superficial, sometimes even misleading. I think we have an obligation to describe the complexities of the programme, including what it is costing and what its results appear to be. And I think we have an obligation to say that we cannot measure these important things as well as people think we can.

C: Well, surely you can be a little less vague as to what you would do. We have been asked to present an evaluation design by a week from next Wednesday. And if we are going to have any pretesting this year we need to get at it next month.

E: I am not trying to be evasive. I prefer gradually developed plans - "progressive focusing" Parlett and Hamilton call it. I would not feel pressed by the deadline. I would perhaps present a sketch like this one (drawing some papers from a folder); one which Les McLean used in the evaluation of an instant-access film facility. His early emphasis was on finding out what issues most concern the people in and around the project.

C: I think of that as the Programme Director's job.

E: Yes, and the evaluation study might be thought of - in part - as helping the Programme Director with his job.

C: Hmmm. It is the Secretary I was thinking we would be helping. You made the point that different people need different information, but it seems to me that you are avoiding the information that the Secretary and many other people want.

E: Let's talk a bit about what the Secretary, or any responsible official, wants. I am not going to presume that a cost-effectiveness ratio is what he wants, or what he would find useful. We may decide later that it is.

First of all, I think that what a responsible official wants in this situation is evidence that the National Programme people are carrying out their contract, that the responsibility for developing new teaching techniques continues to be well placed, and that objectionable departures from the norms of professional work are not occurring.

Second, I think a responsible official wants information that can be used in discussions about policy and tactics.

Our evaluation methodology is not refined enough to give cost-effectiveness statements that policy-setters or managers can use. The conditionality of our ratios and our projections is formidable. What we can do is acquaint decision-makers with this particular programme, with its activities and its statistics, in a way that permits them to relate it to their experiences with other programmes. We do not have the competence to manage educational programmes by ratios and projections — management is still an art. Maybe it should remain an art — but for the time being we must accept it as a highly particularized and judgmental art.

C: I agree — in part. Many evaluation studies are too enormously detailed for effective use by decision-makers. Many of the variables they use are simplistic, even though they show us how their variables correlate with less simplistic measures. Some studies ignore the unrealistic arrangements that are made as experimental controls. But those objectionable features do not make it right to de-emphasize measurement. The fact that management is an art does not mean that managers should avoid good technical information.

What I want from an evaluation is a good reading — using the best techniques available — a good reading of the principal costs and of the principal benefits. I have no doubt that the evaluation methodology we have now is sufficient for us to show people in government, in the schools, and in the general public what the programme has accomplished.

E: If I were to be your evaluator I would get you that reading. I would use the best measures of resource allocation, and of teaching effort, and of student problem-solving we can find. But I would be honest in reporting the limitations of those measures. And I would find other ways also of observing and reporting the accomplishments and the problems of the National Programme.

C: That of course is fair. I do not want to avoid whatever real problems there may be. I do want to avoid collecting opinions as to what problems (and accomplishments) there might be. I want good data. I want neither balderdash nor gossip. I want my questions answered and I want the Secretary's questions answered.

And those questions might change as we go along. You would call that "formative evaluation"?

E: Sometimes. I would also call it "responsive".

C: What kind of final report would you prepare for us?

E: I brought along a couple of examples of previous reports. I can leave them with you. I can provide other examples if you would like. Whether there is a comprehensive or brief final report, whether there is one or several, those decisions can be made later.

C: No, I'm afraid that simply won't do. If we are to commit funds to an evaluation study, we must have a clear idea in advance of how long it is going to take, what it will cost, and what kind of product to expect. That does not mean that we could not change our agreement later.

E: If you need a promise at the outset, we can make it. Believe me, I do not believe it is in your best interests to put a lot of specifications into the "contract". I would urge you to choose your evaluator in terms of how well he has satisfied his previous clients more than on the promises he would make so early.

C: It would be irresponsible of me not to have a commitment from him.

E: Of course. And your evaluator should take some of the initiative in proposing what should be specified and what options should be left open.

C: Let me be frank about one worry I have. I am afraid I may get an evaluator who is going to use our funding to "piggy-back" a research project he has been wanting to do. He might agree to do "our" evaluation study but it might have very little to do with the key decisions of the Experimental Teaching Programme.

E: It is reasonable to expect any investigator to continue old interests in new surroundings. When you buy him you buy his curiosities. He may develop hypotheses, for example, about problem solving and teaching style, hypotheses that sound most relevant to the programme - but the test of these hypotheses may be of little use to those who sponsor, operate, or benefit from the programme.

His favourite tactics, a carefully controlled comparative research effort or a historical longitudinal research study, for example, might be attractive to your staff. But he is not inclined to talk about how unnecessary this approach may be. The inertia in his past work may be too strong. You are right, there is a danger. I think it can best be handled by looking at the assignments the evaluator has had before, and by getting him to say carefully what he is doing and why, and by the sponsor saying very carefully which he wants and does not want, and by everybody being sceptical as to the value of each undertaking, and suggesting alternatives.

C: Would you anticipate publishing the evaluation study in a professional journal?

E: Even when an article or book is desired it is rare for an evaluation study to be suitable for the professional market. Evaluation studies are too long, too multi-purposive, too non-generalizable and too dull for most editors. Research activities within the evaluation project sometimes are suitable for an audience of researchers.

I usually suppose that my evaluation work is not done for that purpose. If something worth publishing became apparent I would talk over the possibilities with you.

C: I think something like that should be in writing. What other assurances can you give me that you would not take advantage of us? Do you operate with some specific "rules of confidentiality"?

E: I would have no objection to a contract saying that I would not release findings about the project without your authorization. I consider the teachers, administrators, parents and children also have rights here. Sometimes I will want to get a formal release from them. Sometimes I will rely on my judgment as to what should and should not be made public, or even passed along to you. In most regards I would follow your wishes. If I should find that you are a scoundrel, and it is relevant to my evaluation studies, I will break my contract and pass the word along to those whom I believe should know.

C: *I* have nothing to lose, but others involved may have. I do not want to sanction scurrilous muck-raking in the name of independent evaluation. I wonder if you are too ready to depend on your own judgment. What if it is you who are the scoundrel?

E: I would expect you to expose me.

C: By exposing you I would be exposing my bad judgment in selecting you - the line of thought I would return to is the safeguard you would offer us against mismanagement of the evaluation study.

E: The main safeguard, I think, is what I was offering at the beginning: communication and negotiation. In day to day matters I make many decisions, but not alone. My colleagues, my sponsors, my information sources help make those decisions. A good contract helps, but it should leave room for new responsibilities to be exercised. It should help assure us that we will get together frequently and talk about what the evaluation study is doing and what it should be doing.

C: What about your quickness to look for problems in the programme? Perhaps you consider your own judgment a bit too precious.

E: I do not think so. Perhaps. I try to get confirmation from those I work with and from those who see things very differently than I do. I deliberately look for disconfirmation of the judgments I make and the judgments I gather from others. If you are thinking about the judgments of what is bad teaching and learning I try to gather the judgments of people both who are more expert than I and those who have a greater stake in it than I. I cannot help but show some of my judgments, but I will look for hard data that support my judgment and I will look just as hard for evidence that runs counter to my opinion.

C: That was nicely said. I did not mean to be rude.

E: You speak of a problem that cuts deeply. There are few dependable checks on an evaluator's judgment. I recognise that.

C: You would use consultation with the project staff and with me, as a form of check and balance.

E: Yes. And I think that you would feel assured by the demands I place upon myself for corroboration and cross-examination of findings.

C: Well, there seems to me to be a gap in the middle. You have talked about how we would look for problems and how you would treat findings - but will there be any findings? What will the study yield?

E: If I were to be your evaluator we might start by identifying some of the key aims, issues, arrangements, activities, people, etc. We would ask ourselves what decisions are forthcoming, what information would we like to have. I would check these ideas with the programme staff. I would ask you and them to look over some things I and other evaluators have done in the past, and say what looks worth doing. The problem would soon be too big a muddle, and we would have to start our diet.

C: I don't care much for the metaphor.

E: That may be as good a basis as any for rejecting an evaluator - his bad choice of metaphors.

C: I've just realized how late it is. I am hoping not to be rejecting any evaluators today. Perhaps you would be willing to continue this later.

E: Let me make a proposal. I appreciate the immediacy of the situation. I know a young woman with a doctorate and research experience, who might be available to co-ordinate the evaluation work. If so, I could probably be persuaded to be the director, on a quarter-time basis. Let me go over your materials with her. We would prepare a sketch of an evaluation plan, and show it to you along with some examples of her previous work.

C: That is a nice offer. Let me look at your examples and think about it before you go ahead. Would it be all right if I called you first thing tomorrow morning? Good. Thanks very much for coming by.

## Commentary on the Conversation with a Responsive Evaluator

I recognised as I started to develop this conversation that the negotiating conditions that I had experienced and the rhetoric I was familiar with were not common in other countries. I felt that the tenacious reader could overcome those parochial features to get at issues that are common to evaluation of large-scale programmes anywhere.

Many readers would prefer a listing of issues rather than a dialogue; I agree that listings can be helpful. I do believe that issues take on a different meaning when they are presented in natural discourse, and that it is useful for practitioners and theorists alike to give attention to these different meanings. The interweaving of pride, vulnerability, aspiration, and other personal and political characteristics into educational purpose and method are more apparent in such discourse than in such a checklist as I presented earlier.

I wanted to keep it a two-person, informal situation for simplicity and because I guessed that that would be most common in Europe. In the U.S.A. open bidding for evaluation contracts is required by law for many national and state programmes. The negotiations have become formal, legalistic, often impersonal, with little attention to the issues raised in this dialogue. Since I was too unfamiliar with any European setting and frame of mind I kept the idea of a conversation but made it an American scenario.

I sent an early draft of this conversation to the following persons for comments, particularly as to how the Commissioner might respond:

Heinrich Bauersfeld
Mathematics Curriculum Developer
University of Bielefeld

Joseph M. Cronin
Secretary of Educational Affairs
State of Massachusetts

Astrid Nyström
National Board of Education
Stockholm

Nils-Eric Svensson,
Executive Director
Stiftelsen Riksbankens
  Jubileumsfond
Stockholm

R.A. Becher
Nuffield Foundation
London

Robert Glasser, Co-Director
Learning Research and Development
  Center
University of Pittsburgh

Lawrence Stenhouse, Director
Centre for Applied Research in
  Education
University of East Anglia

Marc Tucker
National Institute of Education
Washington, D.C.

Most of these respondents found the issues relevant and difficult to resolve. Most noted the discrepancies between their real situations and the fictitious situation. I used many of the wordings they suggested in revising the dialogue. Most of them wanted a quicker declaration of purposes and plans, but my responsive evaluator is convinced that many of the shortcomings of evaluation studies are traced to a willingness to guess at what the key variables and issues are and to make an irretrievable commitment to personnel and instrumentation. And so he is vague, but explorative; anxious to base his worthiness on past performance rather than on what he might promise at present. It is not a stance that all the respondents found persuasive. Some of the reactions of the eight administrators named above are most insightful. I quote a sample of these reactions:

> "Now, if this were my country the project leader would probably not be so free to make his own decisions. They would have been made at a 'higher' level."
>
> "Over here a project director has to fight to get his project evaluated."
>
> "...how clearly this conversation brought out the differing assumptions made in the U.S. from those which would be made in this country – for example, that funds are normally made available under contract, that such contracts stipulate the need for evaluation, and that they impose tight deadlines."
>
> "The dialogue presupposes that the evaluator is a well-known person,...A minor researcher, on his way up,...might expect to be treated with more firmness and prejudice by the commissioner."

"I read your hypothetical conversation over and over again, and (I found the evaluator) too damn patronizing."

"It is necessary to clarify the project philosophy. What really shall be improved? ...the teaching of fractions, the sensitivity of the teacher, the degree of variety/differentiatedness, the style of interaction between teacher and students, or what else?"

"It should be more 'product'-oriented, a typical concern of action administrators."

"The commissioner might probe more to find out if the evaluator is really sympathetic to the programme, shares the values of the creators, thinks it has promise, is willing to concentrate on the goals and variables important to the project staff, shares with the project staff some agreement as to what might be valid indicators of project success."

"Many commissioners would (want) the evaluator to present results...which go along with (their) own interests, or those of the decision makers at higher levels. The Commissioner might discard the evaluator as soon as he realizes that the desired results cannot be bought so easily."

"I would have had the commissioner more tough-minded...raising questions about time span, costs, and scope of the evaluation; the experience and qualifications of the evaluator; the 'subjectivity' of the proposed evidence, the apparent untidiness of the evaluation design, and whether the evaluator's report will offer recommendations about the continuance or discontinuance of the experiment."

"The commissioner might press for what the evaluator means by 'usefulness'...is it the furtherance of science, of psychological methods, of parent insight, of the manipulative power of steering board members, of the child's self awareness, of...? If the evaluator tries to serve all these needs, he is overburdened and soon will become a distractor and an explosive power in the project."

"The point is: How much do the commissioner and evaluator join the common insincerity of producing designs to which they do not stand by?"

"The commissioner might well want to know how much time of how many people with what kind of experience and training will be required, and at what cost."

"Recognition should be made of the fact that commissioners do have particular constituencies and that a wise evaluation would help meet the questions of these constituencies, at the same time getting on with the problems that may lie deeper."

"The commissioner might want to know whether the evaluator's preliminary observations will be available to project staff as the project proceeds, whether such views will be available to others, and what control he will have over premature release of findings."

"The commissioner might want some 'right of reply' to negative findings, whenever they are released, or a chance to confer with the evaluator on the basis of draft reports before the final reports are published."

"The commissioner might want to know how disruptive the evaluator will be, how much time of project staff he will take, whether he can make use of measures routinely administered, whether he will demand the use of control groups, etc."

"If the evaluator's racial, ethnic, or cultural background are different from staff and students, the commissioner might try to find out if the evaluator sees those differences as a problem, and, if so, what the evaluator would propose to do about it."

"Is it not too egotistical to 'learn as much as we can from the project'? Such an outcome is the byproduct of the project, too often the only worthwhile one. A foundation will hardly pay millions for the learnings of the project staff and evaluators."

"I would have suggested some additional issues, such as that of access to participating schools; information about the project's underlying aims; the right to confidentiality of participants in the programme, and the concern for 'proof', rather than evidence, of success or failure."

"I don't think our evaluators have audiences. They have to create them."

Most of these respondents felt that more should have been accomplished in that hypothetical meeting of commissioner and evaluator. Most thought that it was realistic and included some of the more important issues that need to be resolved in such a negotiation.

## A conversation between a person who is commissioning an independent evaluation study and the evaluator who favours a "goal-free" approach

C: Well, we're very glad you were able to take this on for us. We consider this programme in reading for the disadvantaged to be one of the most important we have ever funded. I expect you'd like to get together with the project staff as soon as possible - the director is here now - and of course, there's quite a collection of documents covering the background of the project that you'll need. We've assembled a set of these for you to take back with you tonight.

E: Thanks, but I think I'll pass on meeting the staff and on the materials. I _will_ have my secretary get in touch with the director soon, though, if you can give me the phone numbers.

C: You mean you're planning to see them _later_? But you've got so little time - we thought that bringing the director in would really speed things up. Maybe you'd _better_ see him - I'm afraid he'll be pretty upset about making the trip for nothing. Besides, he's understandably nervous about the whole evaluation. I think his team is worried that you won't really appreciate their approach unless you spend a good deal of time with them.

E: Unfortunately, I can't _both_ evaluate their achievements with reasonable objectivity and also go through a lengthy indoctrination session with them.

C: Well, surely you want to know what they are trying to do - what's _distinctive_ about their approach?

E: I already know more than I need to know about their goals - teaching reading to disadvantaged youngsters, right?

C: But that's so vague - why, they developed their own instruments, and a _very_ detailed curriculum. You can't cut yourself off from _that_! Otherwise, you'll finish up criticizing them for failing to do what they never tried to do. I can't let you do that. In fact, I'm getting a little nervous about letting you go any further with the whole thing. Aren't you going to see them _at all_? You're proposing to evaluate a three million dollar project without even _looking_ at it?

E: As far as possible, yes. Of course, I'm handicapped by being brought in so late and under a tight deadline, so I may have to make some compromises. On the general issue, I think you're suffering from some misconception about evaluation. You're used to the rather cozy relationship which often - in my view - contaminates the objectivity of the evaluator. You should think about the evaluation of drugs by the double-blind approach...

C: But even there, the evaluator has to know the intended effect of the drug in order to set up the tests. In the educational field, it's much harder to pin down goals and that's where you'll <u>have</u> to get together with the developers.

E: The drug evaluator and the educational evaluator do not even have to know the <u>direction</u> of the intended effect, stated in very general terms, let alone the intended extent of success. It's the evaluator's job to <u>find out</u> what effects the drug has, and to assess them. If (s)he is told in which direction to look, that's a handy hint but it's potentially prejudicial. One of the evaluator's most useful contributions may be to reconceptualize the effects, rather than regurgitating the experimenter's conception of them.

C: This is too far-out altogether. What are you suggesting the evaluator do - test for effects on every possible variable? He can't do that.

E: Oh, but he has to do that <u>anyway</u>. I'm not adding to his burden. How do you suppose he picks up side effects? Asks the experimenter for a list? That <u>would</u> be cozy. It's the evaluator's job to look out for effects the experimenter (or producer etc.) <u>did not expect or notice</u>. The so-called "side effects", whether good or bad, often wholly determine the outcome of the evaluation. It's absolutely irrelevant to the evaluator whether these are "side" or "main" effects; that language refers to the <u>intentions</u> of the producer and the evaluator isn't evaluating intentions but <u>achievements</u>. In fact, it's risky to hear even general descriptions of the intentions, because it focuses your attention away from the "side-effects" and tends to make you overlook or down weight them.

C: You still haven't answered the <u>practical</u> question. You can't test for all possible effects. So this posture is absurd. It's much more useful to tell the producer how well he's achieved what he set out to achieve.

E: The producer undoubtedly set out to do something really worthwhile in education. That's the really significant formulation of his goals and it's to that formulation the evaluator must address himself. There's also a highly particularized description of the goals - or there should be - and the producer may need some technical help in deciding whether he got there, but that certainly isn't what <u>you</u>, as the dispenser of taxpayer's funds, need to know. You need to know if the money was wasted or well-spent etc.

C: Look, I already _had_ advice on the goals. That's what my advisory panel tells me when it recommends which proposal to fund. What I'm paying _you_ for is to judge success, not legitimacy of the direction of effort.

E: Unfortunately for that way of dividing the pie, your panel can't tell what _configuration_ of actual effects would result, and that's what I'm here to assess. Moreover, your panel is just part of the whole process that led to this product. They're not immune to criticism, nor are you, and nor is the producer. (And nor am I.) Right now, you have - with assistance - produced something, and I am going to try to determine whether it has any merit. When I've produced my evaluation, you can switch roles and evaluate _it_ - or get someone else to do so. But it's neither possible nor proper for an evaluator to get by without assessing the _merits_ of what has been done, not just its consonance with what someone else thought was meritorious. It isn't proper because it's passing the buck, dodging the - or one of the - issue(s). It isn't possible because (it's almost certain that) no one else _has_ laid down the merits of what has _actually_ happened. It's very unlikely, you'll agree, that the producer has achieved exactly the original goals, without shortfall, overrun or side-effects. So - unless you want to abrogate the contract we just signed - you really have to face the fact that I shall be passing on the _merits_ of whatever has been done - as well as determining exactly what that is.

C: I'm thinking of at least getting someone else in to do it too - someone with a less peculiar notion of evaluation.

E: I certainly hope you do. There's very little evidence about the interjudge reliability of evaluators. I would of course cooperate fully in any such arrangement by refraining from any communication whatsoever with the other evaluator.

C: I'm beginning to get the feeling you get paid rather well for speaking to no one. Will you kindly explain how you're going to check on all variables? Or are you going to take advantage of the fact that I have told you it's a reading programme - I'm beginning to feel that I let slip some classified information. What's your idea of an ideal evaluation situation - one where you don't know what you're evaluating?

E: In evaluation, blind is beautiful. Remember that Justice herself is blind, and good medical research is double blind. The educational evaluator is severely handicapped by the impossibility of double-blind conditions in most educational contexts. But (s)he must still work very hard at keeping out prejudicial information. You can't do an evaluation without knowing what it is you're supposed to evaluate - the treatment - but you do not need or want to know what it's supposed to do. You've already told me too much in that direction. I still need to know some things about the nature of the treatment itself, and I'll find those out from the director, via my secretary, who can filter out surplus data on intentions etc. before relaying it to me. That data on the treatment is what cuts the problem down to size; I have the knowledge about probable or possible effects of treatments like that, from the research literature, that enables me to avoid the necessity for examining all possible variants.

C: Given the weakness of research in this area, aren't you still pretty vulnerable to missing an unprecedented effect?

E: Somewhat, but I have a series of procedures for picking these up, from participant observation to teacher interview to sampling from a list of educational variables. I don't doubt I slip up, too; but I'm willing to bet I miss less than anyone sloshing through the swamp towards goal-achievement. I really think you should hire someone else to do it independently.

C: We really don't have the budget for it...maybe you can do something your way. But I don't know how I'm going to reassure the project staff. This is going to seem a very alien, threatening kind of approach to them, I'm afraid.

E: People that feel threatened by referees who won't accept their hospitality don't understand about impartiality. This isn't support for the enemy, it's neutrality. I don't want to penalize them for failing to reach over-ambitious goals. I want to give them credit for doing something worthwhile in getting halfway to those goals. I don't want to restrict them to credit for their announced contracts. Educators often do more good in unexpected directions than the intended ones. My approach preserves their chance in those directions. In my experience, interviews with project staff are excessively concerned with explanations of shortfall. But shortfall has no significance for me at all. It has some for you, because it's a measure of the reliability of the projections they make in the future. If I were evaluating them as a production team, I'd look at that as part of the track record. But right now I'm evaluating their product - a reading programme. And it may be the best in the world even if it's only half as good as they intended. No, I'm not working in a way that's prejudiced against them.

C: I'm still haunted by a feeling this is an unrealistic approach. For example, how the devil would I ever know who to get as an evaluator except in terms of goal-loaded descriptions. I got you - in fact, I invited you on the phone - to handle a "reading programme for disadvantaged kids" which is goal-loaded. I couldn't even have worked out whether you'd had any experience in this area except by using that description. Do you think evaluators should be <u>universal</u> geniuses? How can they avoid goal-laden language in describing themselves?

E: There's nothing wrong with classifying evaluators by their <u>past</u> performance. You only risk contamination when you tell them what you want them to do <u>this</u> time, using the goals of <u>this</u> project as you do so. There's nothing unrealistic about the alternative, any more than there is about cutting names off scientific papers when you, as an editor, send them out to be refereed. You could perfectly well have asked me if I was free to take on an evaluation task in an area of previous experience - a particularly important one, you could have added - requiring, as it seemed to you, about so much time and with so much fees involved. I could have made a tentative acceptance and then come in to look into details, as I did today.

C: <u>What</u> details can you look at?

E: Sample materials, or descriptions by an observer of the process, availability of controls, time constraints etc. What I found today made it clear you simply wanted the best that could be done in a very limited time, and I took it on that basis - details later. Of course, it probably won't answer some of the crucial evaluation questions, but to do that you should have brought someone in at the beginning. Your best plan would have been to send me reasonably typical materials and tell me how long the treatment runs. That would have let me form my own tentative framework. But no evaluator gets perfect conditions. The trouble is that the loss is not his, it's the consumer's. And that means he's usually not very motivated to preserve his objectivity. It's more fun to be on friendly terms with the project people. By the way, the project I'm on for you <u>is</u> hard to describe concisely in goal-free language, but that's not true in all cases. I often do CAI evaluations, for example, and other educational technology cases, where the description of the project isn't goal-loaded.

C: Look, how long after you've looked at materials before you form a pretty good idea about the goals of the project? Isn't it a bit absurd to fight over hearing it a little earlier?

E: The important question is not whether I do infer the goals but whether I may infer some other possible effects before I am locked-in to a 'set' towards the project's own goals. For example, I've looked at elementary school materials and thought to myself - vocabulary, spelling, general knowledge, two-dimensional representation conventions, book-orientation, reading skills, independent study capacity, and so on. It isn't important which of these is the main goal - if the authors have made any significant headway on it, it will show up; I'm not likely to miss it altogether. And the other dimensions are not masked by your set if you don't have one. Remember that even if a single side-effect doesn't swamp the intended effect, the totality of them may make a very real plus for this programme by comparison with others which do about as well on the intended effect and on cost. After I've looked at materials (not including teachers' handbooks, etc.), I look at their tests. Of course, looking at materials is a little corrupting, too, if you want to talk about pure approaches. What I should really be looking at is students - especially changes in students, and even more especially, changes due to these materials. (I'm quite happy to be looking at their test results, for example.) But the evaluator usually has to work pretty hard before he can establish cause. It's worth realizing, however, that if he had all that, his job is not yet half done. But I guess the most important practical argument for goal-free evaluation is one we haven't touched yet.

C: Namely?

E: I'm afraid there isn't time to go into that now.

Appendix

BIBLIOGRAPHY

ALKIN, Marvin C. Towards an evaluation model: A systems approach. UCLA: Center for the Study of Evaluation, Working Paper No. 4, December, 1967.

ANDERSON, Richard C. The comparative field experiment: An illustration from high school biology. Proceedings of the 1968 Invitational Conference on Testing Problems. Princeton, New Jersey: Educational Testing Service, 1969, 3-30.

BLOOM, Benjamin S., Hastings, J. Thomas, and Madaus, George F. Handbook on formative and summative evaluation of student learning. New York: McGraw-Hill, 1971.

BOERSMA, Wendell C. and Plawecki, Henry M. After the NCA self-evaluation and visitation - what happens? North Central Association Quarterly (5454 South Shore Drive, Chicago), Winter, 1972, XLVI(3), 335-339.

CAMPBELL, Donald. Reforms as experiments. American Psychologist, 1969, 24, 409-429.

CARPENTER, James L. Accreditation evaluation and institutional change. North Central Association Quarterly (5454 South Shore Drive, Chicago), Fall, 1970, XLV(2), 259-263.

COHEN, David K. Politics and research - evaluation of large-scale programs. Review of Educational Research, 1970, 40(2), 213-238.

COLEMAN, James S. Policy research in the social sciences. Morristown, New Jersey: General Learning Press, 250 James Street, 1972.

COLEMAN, James S. et al. Equality of educational opportunity. Washington, D.C.: U.S. Government Printing Office, Supt. of Documents, 1966.

CRONBACH, Lee J. Course improvement through evaluation. Teachers College Record, May, 1963, 64, 672-683. Reprinted in R.W. Heath (Ed.), New Curricula, 1964.

DOUGHTY, Philip L. and Stakenas, Robert G. An analysis of costs and effectiveness of an individualized course in college level geology. In Creta Sabine (Ed.), Accountability: Systems Planning in Education. Homewood, Illinois: ETC Publications, 1973.

DRESSEL, Paul L. Accreditation and institutional self-study. North Central Association Quarterly (5454 South Shore Drive, Chicago), Fall, 1971, XLVI(2), 277-287.

FLEXNER, Abraham. Medical education in the United States and Canada. A report to the Carnegie Foundation for the Advancement of Teaching. New York: The Carnegie Foundation, 1910. Reprinted, New York: Arno Press, 1972.

HAVIGHURST, Robert J. The public schools of Chicago. A survey for the Board of Education of the City of Chicago, 1964.

HEMPHILL, John K. The relationships between research and evaluation studies. In Ralph W. Tyler (Ed.), Educational Evaluation: New Roles, New Means. Chicago: University of Chicago Press, 1969, 68th Yearbook, Part II, National Society for the Study of Education, 189-220.

HOUSE, Ernest, Rivers, Wendell, and Stufflebeam, Daniel. An assessment of the Michigan accountability system. The authors: March, 1974.

HOUSE, Ernest R. and Hogben, Donald. Setting speculative snares. SRIS Quarterly, Spring, 1973, 6(1), 11-13.

HUSEN, Torsten. International study of achievement in mathematics. New York: Wiley, 1967.

JENCKS, Christopher et al. Inequality. New York: Basic Books, 1972.

KNOLL, Robert E. and Brown, Robert D. Experiment at Nebraska: The first two years at a cluster college. University of Nebraska Studies, new series, No. 44. Lincoln: University of Nebraska, June 1972.

KRAFT, Richard H.P. Cost-effectiveness analysis in vocational technical education. AERA Monograph Series on Curriculum Evaluation, Volume 7. Chicago: Rand McNally, 1974.

LESSINGER, Leon M. Accountability for results: A basic challenge for America's schools. In Leon M. Lessinger and Ralph W. Tyler (Eds.), Accountability in Education. Worthington, Ohio: Charles A. Jones, 1971.

LEVINE, Murray. Scientific method and the adversary model: Some preliminary suggestions. Evaluation Comment, 1973, 4(2), 1-3.

LEVITAN, Sar A. *Antipoverty work and training efforts: Goals and reality*. Policy papers in Human Resources and Industrial Relations, Number 3. Ann Arbor: Institute of Labor and Industrial Relations, August, 1967.

LINDVALL, C.M. and Cox, R.C. Evaluation as a tool in curriculum development: The IPI evaluation program. *AERA Monograph Series on Curriculum Evaluation*, Volume 5. Chicago: Rand McNally, 1970.

LUNDGREN, Ulf P. *Frame factors and the teaching process*. Stockholm: Almquist and Wiksell, 1972.

MACDONALD, Barry. Humanities curriculum project. In Schools Council Research Studies, *Evaluation in Curriculum Development: Twelve Case Studies*. London: Macmillan, 1973, 80-90.

MOSTELLER, Frederick and Moynihan, David P. (Eds.) *On equality of educational opportunity*. New York: Vintage Books, 1972.

NATIONAL Study of Secondary school Evaluation. *Evaluative criteria*, fourth edition. Washington, D.C.: National Study, 1785 Massachusetts Avenue, N.W., 20036, 1969.

OWENS, Thomas R. Educational evaluation by adversary proceedings. In Ernest House (Ed.), *School Evaluation - The Politics and Process*. Berkeley: McCutchan Publishing Corporation, 1973.

PARLETT, Malcolm. Study of two experimental programs at MIT. In David Hamilton, Malcolm Parlett, David Jenkins, and Barry MacDonald (Eds.), *Whatever Happened to Daniel Stufflebeam: A Reader in Unconventional Curriculum Evaluation*. New Education Press, in press.

PARLETT, Malcolm and Hamilton, David. *Evaluation as illumination: A new approach to the study of innovatory programs*. Centre for Research in the Educational Sciences, Occasional Paper 9. Edinburgh, Scotland: University of Edinburgh, October, 1972.

PELLA, M., Stanley, Julian C., Wedemeyer, C.A., and Wittich, W.A. The uses of the White films in the teaching of physics. *Science Education*, 46, 6-21.

PLOWDEN, Lady Beatrice et al. A report of the central advisory committee on children and their primary schools. London: Her Majesty's Stationery Office, 1967.

POPHAM, W. James. Objectives and instruction. In Robert Stake (Ed.), *AERA Monograph Series on Curriculum Evaluation*, Volume 3, Instructional Objectives. Chicago: Rand McNally, 1969, 32-64.

PROVUS, Malcolm. *Discrepancy evaluation*. Berkeley: McCutchan, 1973.

REINHARD, Diane L. Methodology development for input evaluation using advocate and design teams. PhD dissertation, Ohio State University, 1972.

RIPPEY, Robert (Ed.) Studies in transactional evaluation. New York: McCutcheon, 1973.

SCRIVEN, Michael. Pros and cons about goal-free evaluation. Evaluation Comment, December, 1972. Also in W. James Popham (Ed.), Evaluation in Education: Current Applications. Berkeley: McCutchan, 1974.

SMITH, Louis M. and Geoffrey, L. The complexities of an urban classroom: An analysis toward a general theory of teaching. New York: Holt, Rinehart, and Winston, Inc., 1968.

SMITH, Louis M. and Pohland, Paul A. Education, technology, and the rural highlands. AERA Monograph Series on Curriculum Evaluation, Volume 7. Chicago: Rand McNally, 1974.

STAKE, Robert E. and Gjerde, Craig. An evaluation of TCITY, the Twin City Institute for Talented Youth. AERA Monograph Series on Curriculum Evaluation, Volume 7. Chicago: Rand McNally, 1974.

STAKE, Robert E. The measuring of education. Berkeley: McCutchan, in press.

STANLEY, Julian C. Controlled field experiments as a model for evaluation. In Peter H. Rossi and Walter Williams (Eds.), Evaluating Social Programs. New York: Seminar Press, 1972, 67-71.

STEELE, Joe M. Arranging field tests: Characteristics of sites and students. Formative Evaluation Report No. 1. Boulder, Colorado: Biological Sciences Curriculum Study, June, 1973.

STUFFLEBEAM, Daniel L. et al. Educational evaluation and decision-making. Itasca, Illinois: Peacock, 1971.

TABA, Hilda. Teaching strategies and cognitive functioning in elementary school children. Cooperative Research Project No. 2404. San Francisco: San Francisco State College, February, 1966.

THOMAS, J. Alan. Cost-benefit analysis and the evaluation of educational systems. Proceedings of the 1968 Invitational Conference on Testing Problems. Princeton, New Jersey: Educational Testing Service, 1968.

TRANKELL, Arne. Kvartet Flisan. Stockholm, 1973.

TYLER, Ralph W. Basic principles of curriculum and instruction. Chicago: University of Chicago Press, 1950.

WEISS, Carol H. Evaluation research: Methods of assessing program effectiveness. Englewood Cliffs, New Jersey: Prentice-Hall, Inc., 1972.

WOLF, Robert L.  The application of select legal concepts to educational evaluation.  Unpublished PhD dissertation, University of Illinois, 1974.

WOMER, Frank B. et al.  *National assessment of educational progress, report 1, 1969-70 science: National results*.  Washington, D.C.: U.S. Superintendent of Documents, July, 1970.

ZDEP, Stanley M. and Joyce, Diane.  The Newark-Verona plan for sharing educational opportunity.  PR-69-13.  Princeton, New Jersey: Educational Testing Service, September 1, 1969.

## OECD SALES AGENTS
## DEPOSITAIRES DES PUBLICATIONS DE L'OCDE

**ARGENTINA – ARGENTINE**
Carlos Hirsch S.R.L.,
Florida 165, BUENOS-AIRES.
☎ 33-1787-2391 Y 30-7122

**AUSTRALIA – AUSTRALIE**
International B.C.N. Library Suppliers Pty Ltd.,
161 Sturt St., South MELBOURNE, Vic. 3205.
☎ 69.7601
658 Pittwater Road, BROOKVALE NSW 2100.
☎ 938 2267

**AUSTRIA – AUTRICHE**
Gerold and Co., Graben 31, WIEN 1. ☎ 52.22.35

**BELGIUM – BELGIQUE**
Librairie des Sciences
Coudenberg 76-78, B 1000 BRUXELLES 1.
☎ 512-05-60

**BRAZIL – BRESIL**
Mestre Jou S.A., Rua Guaipà 518,
Caixa Postal 24090, 05089 SAO PAULO 10.
☎ 216-1920
Rua Senador Dantas 19 s/205-6, RIO DE JANEIRO GB. ☎ 232-07. 32

**CANADA**
Publishing Centre/Centre d'édition
Supply and Services Canada/Approvisionnement et Services Canada
270 Albert Street, OTTAWA K1A OS9, Ontario
☎ (613)992-9738

**DENMARK – DANEMARK**
Munksgaards Boghandel
Nørregade 6, 1165 KØBENHAVN K.
☎ (01) 12 69 70

**FINLAND – FINLANDE**
Akateeminen Kirjakauppa
Keskuskatu 1, 00100 HELSINKI 10. ☎ 625.901

**FRANCE**
Bureau des Publications de l'OCDE
2 rue André-Pascal, 75775 PARIS CEDEX 16.
☎ 524.81.67
Principaux correspondants :
13602 AIX-EN-PROVENCE : Librairie de l'Université. ☎ 26.18.08
38000 GRENOBLE : B. Arthaud. ☎ 87.25.11
31000 TOULOUSE : Privat. ☎ 21.09.26

**GERMANY – ALLEMAGNE**
Verlag Weltarchiv G.m.b.H.
D 2000 HAMBURG 36, Neuer Jungfernstieg 21
☎ 040-35-62-500

**GREECE – GRECE**
Librairie Kauffmann, 28 rue du Stade,
ATHENES 132. ☎ 322.21.60

**HONG-KONG**
Government Information Services,
Sales of Publications Office,
1A Garden Road,
☎ H-252281-4

**ICELAND – ISLANDE**
Snaebjörn Jónsson and Co., h.f.,
Hafnarstræti 4 and 9, P.O.B. 1131,
REYKJAVIK. ☎ 13133/14281/11936

**INDIA – INDE**
Oxford Book and Stationery Co. :
NEW DELHI, Scindia House. ☎ 47388
CALCUTTA, 17 Park Street. ☎ 24083

**IRELAND – IRLANDE**
Eason and Son, 40 Lower O'Connell Street,
P.O.B. 42, DUBLIN 1. ☎ 74 39 35

**ISRAEL**
Emanuel Brown :
35 Allenby Road, TEL AVIV. ☎ 51049/54082
also at :
9, Shlomzion Hamalka Street, JERUSALEM.
☎ 234807
48 Nahlath Benjamin Street, TEL AVIV.
☎ 53276

**ITALY – ITALIE**
Libreria Commissionaria Sansoni :
Via Lamarmora 45, 50121 FIRENZE. ☎ 579751
Via Bartolini 29, 20155 MILANO. ☎ 365083
Sous-dépositaires :
Editrice e Libreria Herder,
Piazza Montecitorio 120, 00186 ROMA.
☎ 674628
Libreria Hoepli, Via Hoepli 5, 20121 MILANO.
☎ 865446
Libreria Lattes, Via Garibaldi 3, 10122 TORINO.
☎ 519274
La diffusione delle edizioni OCDE è inoltre assicurata dalle migliori librerie nelle città più importanti.

**JAPAN – JAPON**
OECD Publications Centre,
Akasaka Park Building,
2-3-4 Akasaka,
Minato-ku
TOKYO 107. ☎ 586-2016
Maruzen Company Ltd.,
6 Tori-Nichome Nihonbashi, TOKYO 103,
P.O.B. 5050, Tokyo International 100-31.
☎ 272-7211

**LEBANON – LIBAN**
Documenta Scientifica/Redico
Edison Building, Bliss Street,
P.O.Box 5641, BEIRUT. ☎ 354429 – 344425

**THE NETHERLANDS – PAYS-BAS**
W.P. Van Stockum
Buitenhof 36, DEN HAAG. ☎ 070-65.68.08

**NEW ZEALAND – NOUVELLE-ZELANDE**
The Publications Manager,
Government Printing Office,
WELLINGTON: Mulgrave Street (Private Bag),
World Trade Centre, Cubacade, Cuba Street,
Rutherford House, Lambton Quay ☎ 737-320
AUCKLAND: Rutland Street (P.O.Box 5344)
☎ 32.919
CHRISTCHURCH: 130 Oxford Tce, (Private Bag)
☎ 50.331
HAMILTON: Barton Street (P.O.Box 857)
☎ 80.103
DUNEDIN: T & G Building, Princes Street
(P.O.Box 1104), ☎ 78.294

**NORWAY – NORVEGE**
Johan Grundt Tanums Bokhandel,
Karl Johansgate 41/43, OSLO 1. ☎ 02-332980

**PAKISTAN**
Mirza Book Agency, 65 Shahrah Quaid-E-Azam,
LAHORE 3. ☎ 66839

**PHILIPPINES**
R.M. Garcia Publishing House,
903 Quezon Blvd. Ext., QUEZON CITY,
P.O. Box 1860 – MANILA. ☎ 99.98.47

**PORTUGAL**
Livraria Portugal,
Rua do Carmo 70-74. LISBOA 2. ☎ 360582/3

**SPAIN – ESPAGNE**
Libreria Mundi Prensa
Castelló 37, MADRID-1. ☎ 275.46.55
Libreria Bastinos
Pelayo, 52, BARCELONA 1. ☎ 222.06.00

**SWEDEN – SUEDE**
Fritzes Kungl. Hovbokhandel,
Fredsgatan 2, 11152 STOCKHOLM 16.
☎ 08/23 89 00

**SWITZERLAND – SUISSE**
Librairie Payot, 6 rue Grenus, 1211 GENEVE 11.
☎ 022-31.89.50

**TAIWAN**
Books and Scientific Supplies Services, Ltd.
P.O.B. 83, TAIPEI.

**TURKEY – TURQUIE**
Librairie Hachette,
469 Istiklal Caddesi,
Beyoglu, ISTANBUL, ☎ 44.94.70
et 14 E Ziya Gökalp Caddesi
ANKARA. ☎ 12.10.80

**UNITED KINGDOM – ROYAUME-UNI**
H.M. Stationery Office, P.O.B. 569, LONDON
SE1 9 NH, ☎ 01-928-6977, Ext. 410
or
49 High Holborn
LONDON WC1V 6HB (personal callers)
Branches at: EDINBURGH, BIRMINGHAM,
BRISTOL, MANCHESTER, CARDIFF,
BELFAST.

**UNITED STATES OF AMERICA**
OECD Publications Center, Suite 1207,
1750 Pennsylvania Ave, N.W.
WASHINGTON, D.C. 20006. ☎ (202)298-8755

**VENEZUELA**
Libreria del Este, Avda. F. Miranda 52,
Edificio Galipán, Aptdo. 60 337, CARACAS 106.
☎ 32 23 01/33 26 04/33 24 73

**YUGOSLAVIA – YOUGOSLAVIE**
Jugoslovenska Knjiga, Terazije 27, P.O.B. 36,
BEOGRAD. ☎ 621-992

Les commandes provenant de pays où l'OCDE n'a pas encore désigné de dépositaire peuvent être adressées à :
OCDE, Bureau des Publications, 2 rue André-Pascal, 75775 Paris CEDEX 16
Orders and inquiries from countries where sales agents have not yet been appointed may be sent to
OECD, Publications Office, 2 rue André-Pascal, 75775 Paris CEDEX 16

**OECD PUBLICATIONS, 2, rue André-Pascal, 75775 Paris Cedex 16 - No. 37.267 1976**

PRINTED IN FRANCE